The Ex-Offender's Job Search Companion

(Getting a Good Job Despite Your Record)

By Kathleen Lordan

Contributing Editors:
Scott Eubanks
Lina Ingraham
Denny Keiffer
Julie McKowen
Jim Wolfe

Cover Design: Randy Hamilton

Portions of this workbook have been adapted from *Successful Job Hunting* by Leonard Corwen

To purchase additional copies or for a quote on large quantities contact:

Cambridge Educational
P.O. Box 2153
Charleston, WV 25328-2153
Phone: 1 (800) 468-4227
Fax: 1 800-FAX ON US

ISBN: 1-56450-312-7

Table of Contents

FOREWORD

Finding a job for the average citizen is hard work: hitting the pavement every day, knocking on doors, making phone calls, writing letters, sending out resumes. As you probably realize, with a record, finding a job will be even tougher. So what are your choices? Your choices are to put your best foot forward, open your eyes, and prepare yourself for the best job search campaign possible!

Half the battle in finding a job is working hard on finding a job. The other half is know-how, like getting the education and job skills you need to be marketable. No matter who you are, people with some sort of education and skills will have the advantage over those who don't. The more education and skills you have, the better chance you will have to overcome your past.

If you did not complete high school, it is very important to begin working toward your diploma. Pursuing an education will show employers that you are goal-oriented and motivated, and that you possess basic reading, writing, and math skills. Ask your case worker about getting a diploma or a General Equivalency Diploma (G.E.D.), which is like getting a diploma, but you don't have to go to "high school." A diploma or G.E.D. is very important when you are looking for a job.

Having a job gives a person a tremendous sense of self-esteem. Ex-offenders who do not find work quickly, get frustrated and discouraged and may find themselves slipping into the behavior that caused them trouble in the first place. Try not to lose sight of your goals. Build a support group that will help you through the highs and lows of your job search campaign. Anyone can get down when things don't go their way. Even the best job search campaign results in a lot of rejection. The longer you have to wait, the harder it is to keep a positive attitude. But you must.

This workbook encourages you to focus on finding a job. You are going to work hard, get up early every morning, and implement your job search strategies every day. Don't fall into the routine of the far too typical job hunter who:

- Sleeps late
- Averages four to six hours a week job hunting
- Sees all the latest movies
- Has little direction or focus
- Answers a few classified advertisements
- Has fuzzy objectives or goals
- Registers with one or two employment agencies and waits for the telephone to ring
- Makes a halfhearted attempt at calling some companies
- Is embarrassed to tell anyone he or she is unemployed
- Doesn't follow-up interviews
- Knows all the plots of daytime soap operas

Keep your eyes on your goals. Make a job search plan of what you will do <u>every day</u> for an entire week. The next week, do it again, then again, until you accept a job. With hard work, you're going to find a job and become part of the community. Hundreds of thousands of ex-offenders have found jobs, stayed out of trouble, and gotten on with their lives. You can too!

When it comes to hiring, employers look for: ATTITUDE, ENTHUSIASM, PERSISTENCE, EFFORT and DETERMINATION. These are the traits they will be looking for in you. To be hired, you must work on and demonstrate these skills.

ATTITUDE: Employers believe that an employee's attitude toward his or her job is very important. Do you take pride in your work? Are you willing to go the extra mile to complete a project? Do you possess a positive CAN-DO attitude?

ENTHUSIASM: When your competitor for a job has a college degree and two years more experience, enthusiasm can tip the scales in your favor. If your attitude is, "Mr. Employer, here I am. What can *you* do for *me*?" THE JOB GAME WILL BE OVER BEFORE IT STARTS. Practice saying, "Yes, I can do that." Or, "I'm a quick learner, I'll be able to do that in no time." Your attitude must be "Mr. Employer, here is what I can do to help you. Here is what I can do to contribute to your business."

PERSISTENCE: Remember the saying, "The squeaky wheel gets the grease." If you are persistent in looking for a job, in scheduling appointments with employers, in following up after your interviews, you WILL get a job. Persistence shows you are serious about what you are doing, that you want a job, and you are willing to work very hard to get one.

EFFORT: You must be willing to do whatever is necessary to get a job, no matter how distressing or discouraging it gets. Nothing should be too much for you to do. You must be willing to sacrifice time with your family and friends and put your personal life on hold. Keep your ultimate objective, finding the job you want, at the top of your "to do" list.

DETERMINATION: Don't let anything stop you. And no excuses, such as:

- "No one will hire me because of my record."
- "Things are slow in the summer, no one is hiring."
- "I need a vacation before starting my job hunt. I've been inside too long."
- "I'll start looking after the holidays." (There are always holidays.)
- "There's no rush. I can always find a job."
- "I deserve some time off."
- "The economy is bad."
- "The unemployment rate is eight percent."

You will be faced with making decisions every minute of the day. Excuses will only keep you from achieving your goals. Don't let anything stand in the way of trying to build a better life. There will be frustrations and disappointments. But, let's face it, this may be especially true for those who have a record.

Don't get down if you can't find a job immediately. Most people have been rejected at one time or another. You will have to learn to cope with rejection, too. Finding a job is critical to gaining self-esteem and ultimately, social acceptance. It is the key ingredient to changing the course of your life. Never give up. It only takes <u>one</u> "Okay, we'll give you a try" to be successful. You CAN do it.

Chapter 1

Prepare Now For Tomorrow

If you are still inside the system, there are things you should do to make your return to society easier. If you are already out, you will need to get moving on these things right away. Number One: If you don't have a high school diploma, start working toward your General Equivalency Degree, or G.E.D., now!

A diploma shows you possess basic reading, writing and math skills. This greatly increases your chances of getting a job. A college degree increases your chances even more. The more education you have, the better prepared you will be to take on responsibilities in a new job. Talk to your case worker or parole officer about starting a G.E.D. program today.

Number Two: Obtain proper identification and other records. Certain forms of identification are required before you can be legally employed. Other forms, like work records, certificates, and professional license are very helpful. Some documents you will need are:

Social Security Card—A Social Security Card is required for employment. To obtain a new one or replace a lost card, contact your local Social Security Office. Again, ask your case worker to help you request these forms. They may have the paperwork already in their office. Social Security cards and other forms of identification cannot be sent to inmates; have them sent to your case worker.

Work Experience Records—References may be hard to get from people you knew before you were incarcerated. Did you work while you were incarcerated? Who can provide you with a reference? Get names and addresses of anyone who can help: teachers, employers, ministers. Ask their permission to use them as a reference and make sure it will be a good reference. You will give this list to potential employers so they can call and ask what type of employee you were.

Birth Certificate—When employers hire you, they commonly need two forms of identification for their records. Do you have a birth certificate? If you don't, get a copy by contacting the Bureau of Vital Statistics in the town or city where you were born.

Driver's License—Try to get a regular driver's license as soon as you are released. You may also want to consider studying for a commercial license since many jobs require a commercial permit. You can get a copy of the booklet to study for a commercial license directly from the Motor Vehicle Administration. If your license has been revoked, you may need a copy of your driving record. If you don't drive, you may want to get a State ID card instead. Look in your telephone directory (in the Federal or State Government listings) for the Motor Vehicle Administration office nearest you.

Military Discharge Papers—If you were in the military, you probably held several jobs during your service. Contact the Military Personnel Records Center, 9700 Page Boulevard, St. Louis, Missouri 63132, (314) 263-3901 for your records. These records can show your work history while you were in the military.

Proof of Education—Contact schools you have attended for records of vocational, technical, or college courses, apprenticeship certificates, or training certificates you have received.

Occupational or professional license—If you have obtained a professional license of some kind, make sure it is still up-to-date and valid. The group that issued it to you will be able to tell you if you are still certified.

Alien Registration Card—If you are not a U.S. citizen and you have misplaced your green card, contact your local Immigration and Naturalization Service office. This will be under the Federal Government listings in your telephone directory.

Rap sheet—You should double check your rap sheet when you are released to make sure it is accurate. Mistakes on this form could cost you a job.

Credit report—You may not have charged anything in a while, but your credit report could say differently. Clear up any mistakes on this report as well. Mistakes on this form can prevent you from making purchases on credit. Ask your case worker or parole officer about how to get these records.

Chapter 2

New Kid on the Block

One of the first decisions you will make is for what kind of an organization you want to work. A good many job hunters aim for the giants, the Fortune 500 companies. They get all the publicity and they seem to attract all the money. But are they the best employers? Big is not necessarily best.

Smaller firms and family owned firms are more likely to hire individuals with a record. If you get an interview with a smaller firm, you are likely to be talking with someone with more authority than interviewers in larger firms. Interviewers in smaller firms are less concerned about "taking risks" and are more likely to take a chance on you. In smaller firms you are also less likely to run into "unwritten" policies of not hiring ex-cons.

On the other hand, very small companies can be risky. Although they can grow fast, they can also end fast. Many small firms are family owned and operated, so it can be harder to get hired if you are not one of the family.

If this is your first job search, you may think you are making the most important decision of your life. You are not. Don't overanalyze your choice of a first employer. Job applicants who are afraid of accepting a position that might not be exactly the right one, find themselves looking for something that does not exist - the perfect job. Most never find it.

What IS important is finding a job that fits your skills. To help your job search or to decide what type of training you should pursue, you need to assess what kind of work you would like to do and what kind of jobs you may do best. This means you need to figure out your strengths, weaknesses, interests, and what you really want to do.

What Are Your Strengths?

Your strengths could be general or specific strengths that are related to a job you held previously. General strengths are personal traits: being dependable, cooperative, honest, hard-working, well-organized, efficient, strong, and having good writing skills. Do you possess any of these?

What about specific strengths related to a job? Examples of these would be: operating a cash register, accounts payable, painting, welding, driving a truck, waiting on tables, operating machinery. Do you possess any of these skills?

Assessing these strengths will help you talk about yourself in an interview, on your resume, or in your cover letter.

What Are Your Weaknesses?

Everyone has weaknesses. By knowing yours, you will be prepared to handle them. Is your age a drawback? Do you have a physical weakness? Are you terrible with numbers? What you do to keep your weaknesses from affecting you on the job is just as important as knowing what your strengths are. For example, you wouldn't apply for a job lifting crates in a warehouse if you have a bad back.

What Are Your Interests?

What do you like to do? Are you good with food? Do you like to drive? Do you enjoy doing things with your hands? Use the following exercise to decide what does and does not interest you. Then look for a job that relates to what you like to do. Remember, you will do best at what you really like to do!

What Do You Really Want To Do?

Rule a sheet of paper down the middle. Head the first column "What I Would Like To Do," the second column "What I Would Not Like To Do." In each column list the work by function, not job title. Write down everything that comes to mind, no matter how silly or small it may seem at the moment. Consider the following factors:

- Daily duties
- Responsibilities
- The kind of people I want to work with
- The geographical location of the job
- The industry - private, public, nonprofit
- The product or service
- Skills involved
- Size of the company
- Individual or team activities
- Travel and/or relocation preferences
- Degree of stress or pressure on the job

What I would like to do	What I would not like to do

Prepare a Skills Inventory

Seriously consider this list. Once you have decided what you think you would like to do, match your skills with the list. Do you have the skills to do what you want to do? Do you need more training?

Spend some time going over your present situation, your job preferences, and skills inventory to help decide in which direction to steer your career. With each job goal, you have to promise that you will give it a chance. You have to promise that you will work hard toward your goal and you will not get discouraged and quit.

Setting Your Goals

After you have assessed your strengths, weaknesses, interests, and what you would like to do, it is time to set your goals.

Start by setting a short-term goal. Your short-term goal should be finding your **first** job now that you are out of the system. You need to look at the basics. You will need to match the job to your skills. Is it a good place to get experience? How much does it pay? You will need to figure out how much money you need to live on.

You may have to start at the bottom of the ladder and work your way up. With hard work, many people move up quickly.

Next, make a long-term goal to find a job you like and can do well. This will be the career you are aiming for, one that requires more skills or education and job contacts before you can obtain it. Think about what you must learn to get it and look for opportunities to get you there. Can you take a class or serve an apprenticeship?

Choose your goals realistically. Your short-term goal (a job) should be a stepping-stone to get to your long-term goal (a career).

Use Your Past Job History to Find Your Strengths, Weaknesses & Set Your Goals

You may have a lot more to offer an employer than you think! Keep an open mind about the jobs you have had and the skills you have acquired over the years. Think about each job separately and pull them apart, task by task. Write each task down. For example: If you worked in food preparation, you had to follow recipes and other instructions, meet deadlines, diagnose problems, meet quality standards, and juggle multiple tasks. *You didn't just make food for hungry people.* If you were a custodian, you oversaw the orderliness of the facility, maintained cleaning supplies, and addressed hazardous situations that interfered with efficiently running the facility. *You didn't just push a broom or mop up spills.* Remember to include jobs you had while incarcerated.

Here is how it could be written:

Position: Cook

Tasks: Followed recipes and directions, met quality standards in regards to food and hygiene, prepared several dishes at the same time, worked quickly and efficiently

Position: Custodian

Tasks: Maintained cleaning supplies and orderliness of building, cleaned 24 rooms every shift, worked with hazardous chemicals

Use the space below to list the last four jobs you have had and your responsibilities.

Position 1:   _____

Tasks: _____

                _____

                _____

Position 2:   _____

Tasks: _____

                _____

                _____

Position 3:   _____

Tasks: _____

                _____

                _____

Position 4:   _____

Tasks: _____

                _____

                _____

Don't worry about form or format. Your purpose now is to get everything down on paper, everything you have done, the jobs you have held, your responsibilities, and the importance of those responsibilities to getting a job. You can organize this list later when you start writing your resume.

If your work history shows that you haven't been steadily employed, that you haven't held a job for some time, or that you were fired from a job, you could explain that you have a record and that is why your work history is lacking. Or, you could lie. If you lie, chances are you will be caught. Do not lie.

Ex-offenders have to face this issue. Develop a network of people who can vouch for you and who believe in you. These are people who are willing to say you have turned yourself around and you deserve a second chance.

If you don't have any experience or education, don't be afraid to start at the bottom of an organization. You can move up from wherever you start, and if you work hard, you may move up quickly and gain experience along the way. The more you know, the more valuable you will be to an employer.

Do You Have a Special Interest?

Is there something special you would like to do? Perhaps you need a special training program. Is this possible? How will you support yourself while you are getting this training or education? Can you live with family or friends? Sometimes government programs, apprenticeships, community colleges, or vocational schools offer training that can fit your situation. Contact a guidance or career counselor at a community college or vocational center for help. Your parole officer may also know of special programs.

Closely examine your strengths, weaknesses, what you have done and what you like to do. You will need this information for your resume and for interviews. You may be amazed at how much you really have learned and what you have to offer a prospective employer.

Chapter 3

Starting Your Job Search

Few people really look forward to *searching* for a job, so you are not alone. Where do you start? How do you get there? What is it going to be like once you are in an interviewer's office? What if you say the wrong thing? How can you deal with the incarceration issue?

To begin, develop a plan of action. Don't try to find a job by yourself. Make a plan for getting help. Get as many people to help you as possible. "Who?" Everybody and anybody: parole services, government agencies, community service organizations, and religious groups to name just a few. It is their job to help you find a job. That's right, people like you. People with a record. All you have to do is use these resources. They could become your best friends.

Several resources are almost always available and helpful. Public libraries have a wealth of resources. Most libraries have career centers with books, tapes, and videos on how to get and keep a job. The federal government is centralizing many resources at one stop career centers nationwide. Call your local unemployment office to find the closest resource center. One stop career centers have staff that will coach you, advise you, and assist you in finding a job. You can also get help at most state welfare offices, workforce development offices, Job Corps Centers, and many YMCA/YWCA facilities.

Organizations like these are critical to helping you find a job. You will probably find someone on their staff to support you in all of your efforts. You need someone who will believe in you and help you with job leads and interview techniques. Here are some of the resources you have at hand:

Parole or Probation Office. You will probably report to your probation officer on a regular basis. Your parole officer may be your most important asset and resource. Your parole officer probably keeps a list of local employers known to hire ex-offenders. If they don't keep a written list, they can give you oral recommendations. Furthermore, your parole officer can make a huge difference in your job search success. If you can get your parole officer to take a personal interest in your file (despite being overloaded with other cases), you may have an invaluable asset as part of your job network.

In some states, the parole board can restore certain legal rights to you . If you have only one felony conviction and complete parole without another felony conviction, the parole board can issue you a Certificate of Relief from Disability. If you have more than one felony conviction, but you are straight for a certain period of time, they may be able to issue you a Certificate of Good Conduct. This depends on how severe your crime was. Your parole officer will be able to tell you if this is possible in your case. In some cases, getting one of these certificates may help you get a job because it shows employers that you are serious about changing your life.

Public Employment Service. Most cities have a public employment service, which is an agency where people who are out of work apply for unemployment benefits. Look in your telephone directory under State Government for listings. In some states it is called the job service. These organizations help the unemployed find work. They generally do not have a specific program for ex-offenders, but some do, so ask. Their mission is to help people find jobs. They do this through career counseling, job-search training, teaching resume writing, and helping you realize your skills.

Once they help you identify your skills, they will try to match them with job openings. In particular, they can give you information on two Federal programs that could encourage employers to hire you. One is the Targeted Jobs Tax Credit which gives employers of ex-offenders a tax break for one year. The other is the Federal Bonding Program which provides insurance (protecting the employer from theft or destruction by employees) for people the employer's bonding company will not insure. Your counselor can tell you more about applying for these programs.

JTPA Programs. The Job Training Partnership Act. State and local governments and businesses provide free job training under this program. You must have a low income to qualify. This is a very good program to help with your job search. They will provide you with job search counseling, on-the-job training, and literacy and basic skills training.

Your case worker will know more details. If he or she does not, look in the telephone book in the white pages for Private Industry Council or under city and government listings for Employment and Training or Human Resources.

Community Social Service Agencies. Different agencies exist in every community that will help ex-offenders find jobs. These organizations are supported by state or local government funding or through charitable or even religious groups. You will find listings of these agencies in the Yellow Pages under social services, vocational training and job placement, or crisis intervention.

The Salvation Army is a place you should check into before you leave the system, or at least, add it to your list of places for help when you get out. Many have specific programs to help ex-offenders, but if yours doesn't, they will offer immediate help with temporary lodging and food as well as referrals to other social service agencies.

If you have a drug or alcohol dependency, you will need to get in touch with your local **Alcoholics Anonymous** or **Narcotics Anonymous** programs. These organizations can be found in the white pages of your phone book.

Take advantage of the agencies in your community. Many of them are staffed by ex-offenders who will understand your situation and what you are going through. You will find a strong support group to help you get your life back together. These counselors will help you find the program you need—for job training, to improve your reading and writing skills, to help you prepare for the G.E.D exam or for substance abuse counseling.

Chapter 4

Where The Jobs Are

Many jobs are not advertised and not listed with employment agencies. Frequently job candidates come from within the company. Most firms look to their present staff before going public with job openings. Some large firms have established policies requiring the posting of new jobs so that current employees have the opportunity to apply first.

To get a job, you must be able to attract the attention of the manager who makes the hiring decisions. There are several ways you can do this.

1.   You can hire the Goodyear blimp to fly your resume in front of the manager's window.
2.   You can hand your resume out to everyone who passes you on the street.
3.   You can conduct a direct mail campaign to market your experience, skills, and accomplishments.

Plan #1 will get you a story in the newspaper and a certain amount of press, which should last about two days. But, it won't get you a job.
Plan #2 will require a lot of resumes.
Plan #3 will get you interviews.

The four key elements of a successful direct marketing campaign are:

The right list of companies
Your cover letter and resume
The interview
Follow-up

Where To Look For Leads

A list of job possibilities will get your job search started. The following table lists jobs that can be done by many workers who have no more than 12 years of education. This list also shows where many of these workers are employed. Where you live it may be different, but this table offers a close picture of most of the jobs you may be able to get. Keep in mind, some of these jobs may require a special license or certificate.

Make sure you check for restrictions on jobs. Ex-offenders are often barred from health-related jobs because of the easy access to drugs. Ex-offenders may also be barred from any jobs related to their crime. Someone convicted of stealing cash, for example, will not be able to work as a bank teller or cashier.

Occupation	Type of Employer
Auto Body Repairer	Car dealerships, car repair shops, paint shops, rental car agencies.
Auto Mechanic	Gas stations, car dealerships, service stations, car factories, larger companies with their own fleets.
Barber and cosmetologist	Beauty shops, department store hair salons, hospitals, hotels, cosmetic counters in stores, retirement homes.
Billing Clerk	Insurance companies, warehouses, stores, radio and television stations, telephone, utility companies.
Bookkeeping Clerk	Warehouses, stores, schools.
Building Maintenance	Apartment complexes, schools, hospitals, office buildings, factories, government offices.
Bus Driver	Buslines, schools, tour bus companies.
Butcher and Meat Cutter	Grocery stores, butcher shops, meat and poultry processing factories, meat and fish markets.
Carpenter	Construction companies, home improvement stores, local unions.
Cashier	Grocery stores, retail stores, department stores, convenience stores, gas stations.
Chef and cook	Restaurants, hotels, resorts, catering businesses, cafeterias, schools, hospitals.
Construction	State government agencies, construction companies, local unions.
Dining Room and Cafeteria Attendant and Buser	Cafeterias, restaurants, catering businesses, bowling alleys, country clubs.
Driver-sales Worker or Route Driver	Delivery companies, grocery stores, special delivery, florists, drycleaners, newspapers.

Occupation	Type of Employer
Electrician	Construction companies, contracting firms, local unions.
Farm Worker	Farms.
File Clerk	Law office, government office or insurance agency. Mainly secretarial.
Food Counter Clerk	Fast food restaurants, coffee shops, cafeterias, grocery stores, convenience stores.
Food Preparation Worker	Grocery stores, restaurants, catering businesses, hotels, hospitals, schools, country clubs.
Freight, Stock and Material Handler	Factories, construction companies, warehouses, grocery stores, trucking companies.
Gardener and Groundskeeper	Individual homes, nurseries, parks, golf courses, cemeteries, race tracks, hotels, garden stores, amusement parks.
Gas Station Attendant	Gas and service stations.
General Office Clerk	Any place where you receive, ship, or mail packages. Companies with a warehouse, a factory, a retail store, direct mail outlet.
Hand Packer	Factories, warehouses, stores.
Industrial Forklift and Tractor Operator	Factories, construction companies, trucking companies, warehouses.
Industrial Machinery Repairer	Work in factories repairing equipment for food processing, transportation, textiles, metal products; gas and electric companies.
Institution or Cafeteria Cook	Hospitals, schools, universities, government, large companies.
Janitor and Custodian	Schools, buildings, government, companies, apartment buildings, churches, factories.

Occupation	Type of Employer
Machinist	Factories where you make small engine aircraft, cars, industrial machinery.
Metal/Plastics-Working Machine Operator	Factories that make metal or plastic parts ranging from light switch plates to truck bed covers.
Painter	Government contractors, schools, hospitals, factories, interior design groups, local unions. Many are self-employed.
Plumber	Mechanical and plumbing contractors, petroleum and chemical plants, factories, local unions.
Precision Assembler	Factories that make electrical or electronic parts such as electrical switches, radios, phones, televisions. Factories that make farm equipment, construction equipment, office machines, motor vehicles.
Private Household Worker	Private homes: gardening, baby-sitting, cleaning, elderly care, mowing, driving.
Retail Sales Worker	Any place where products are sold. Clothing, shoes, music, jewelry, cars, food, computers, office supplies, furniture, etc.
Sewing Machine Operator	Clothing and textile factories, laundry and dry cleaning stores, clothing stores, alteration departments.
Sheet Metal Worker and Duct Installer	Plumbing, heating and air-conditioning contractors, roofing and sheet-metal contractors.
Shipping Clerk	Mainly secretarial. All types of companies need general office help.
Short Order and Fast Food Cook	Fast food restaurants, bars, coffee shops, diners.
Stock Clerk	Department stores, groceries, factories, parts stores, warehouses, any place where merchandise is kept.

Occupation	Type of Employer
Occupation	**Type of Employer**
Truck Driver	Trucking companies, warehouses, oil companies, lumber yards, food and grocery distributors, auto parts stores.
Typist and Word Processor	Mainly secretarial. Government work, schools, insurance offices, receptionists, law offices. May have to be able to type a certain number of words per minute.
Waiter and Waitress	Restaurants, bars, catering businesses, coffee shops, clubs.
Welder	Places that make machinery, cars, planes, boats, bridges, buildings, pipelines, local unions.
Woodworker	Sawmills, lumber yards, furniture stores, repair shops, furniture factories, millwork.

Chapter 5

Job Search Tools

Traditional vs. Nontraditional Tools

You can use several types of tools to find a job—some are a lot more effective than others. You can read classified ads, send out hundreds of resumes, look for help-wanted signs in store windows, or sign up with a local employment agency. These are common, or traditional, tools that are used by many job seekers. Traditional tools have been used for years because they require a minimal investment of time and effort. Unfortunately, methods requiring the least time and effort tend to bring the least effective results.

Users of traditional tools wait for things to happen—an appropriate job to appear in the classified ads, a response to a resume, a phone call about an application. Most of the successful applicants don't find jobs this way because the majority of desirable positions are not advertised. With so many applicants entering the work force, many employers either don't want or don't need to advertise. Think of how many job applicants like you are out there answering ads. That's a lot of competition! Waiting for a response to your resume will not help you find a job. This doesn't mean that no one can find a job this way, but the chances of finding a job using only traditional tools are slim. The most effective job search tools are proactive-not reactive. That means taking action!

A proactive job search begins by using nontraditional tools such as networking and informational interviewing. Networking is enlisting everyone you know to help you with your job search. Informational interviewing is meeting people in the industry, learning about their particular fields, and getting your name in the public eye. You contact the employers. You arrange the interviews. You follow-up on your actions. With nontraditional tools, you have control over the direction of your job search. Resumes and cover letters are still important to your job search, but it will be nontraditional tools like networking and informational interviewing that will make you stand out above the rest. If you are going to make the most of your job search efforts, you should investigate every job lead you receive, and that means combining nontraditional tools with traditional tools.

Nontraditional job search techniques are even more effective when you have an obstacle to overcome, such as a police record, incarceration, or a physical or mental handicap. If you face any of these obstacles in your job search, nontraditional job search techniques allow you to create ways to overcome these obstacles.

Make A Plan

Looking for a job requires effort as well as patience—it could take months to find one. But if you make a plan of action and use both nontraditional and traditional job search tools, your hard work will enable you to find a job that is right for you. Don't just rush into your campaign. You

need to be organized. Make a plan of what you are going to accomplish every day. For many of you, that means your job search has just gone from one of reaction to proaction. You will use every job search tool available to you and properly follow up. That may sound frightening, but don't worry. This workbook not only explains the benefits of important tools, but also shows you how to keep track of them.

Use Your Creativity

Countless books and guides have been written on how to conduct your job search. Knowing how to conduct a job search could mean the difference between finding "a" job and finding "THE" job you want. This workbook explains job search tools that have been successful for candidates in the past and encourages you to take an active role in finding the job you want. You may have your own ideas on how to conduct your job search. This workbook is just a guide. Be creative. There is no one and only absolute way to launch your job search. Do what works for you!

Chapter 6

Nontraditional Tools

Nontraditional tools, such as networking, informational interviewing, and using the Internet get as many people involved in your job search as possible. Rather than making you wait for things to happen, nontraditional tools create opportunities.

Nontraditional tools increase your chances of finding a job by helping you meet professionals in the industry, learn more about a particular field, and increase the number of people who can help you in your search. Nontraditional tools encourage initiative and drive while making **you stand out** in a crowd of applicants. You will learn more about your chosen industry and acquire invaluable **contacts** in the field that interests you. These tools also help **you** take a good **look at your future** and where you would like your career to go by talking to professionals who have already been there. These are characteristics that employers love to see.

Applicants taking an active role in their job search will become employees who take an active role in their jobs and in their companies.

Networking

Networking, as we've discussed, is contacting everyone you know, describing your current job search status, and asking for advice about conducting your job search. That probably seems impossible and intimidating, but it isn't once you learn how to network.

Networking can save you time and help you find a job more easily. Picture this: When you are looking for the best way to get to Dickenson Street from Main Street, what do you do? You might ask someone for directions. What do you do when you are looking for a good restaurant? You ask friends and relatives for recommendations.

When asking these questions, you are networking. Networking is a **shortcut** to finding the information you need by **asking <u>everyone</u> for input and advice.** You don't have time to try all of the alternatives. People are a marvelous source of information! They enjoy being asked what they think!

Let's assume that instead of looking for a restaurant, you're trying to find a job. If you told a few people you were looking for a job, they might give you some advice and tell you anything and everything they know; who's hiring, who you should talk to, and what companies you should contact. What a tremendous time saver! Without a doubt, networking will bring you the best results, more so than if you simply mailed some cover letters and waited for a response. By informing everyone you know that you are looking for a job, you will definitely increase your chances of hearing about, finding, and landing one.

So what is networking? *Networking is telling your friends, neighbors and relatives about your current job search status*. It is **not** asking them for a job. It is an informal way of telling everyone you know what you are interested in doing and that you are ready to start NOW—and then asking them for their advice. Word-of-mouth through acquaintances and associates is the best resource to finding out where the jobs are. Even if you don't know many people, your list will grow in time. Contact the people you know and see if they can refer you to someone else. For every three people you know, your contacts are bound to introduce you to three more.

Networking Objectives

- To uncover hidden job opportunities.
- To increase your contacts and broaden your information network.
- To show you are now a responsible person willing to work hard and be honest.
- To find out more information about the market, a specific company, or a particular field.
- To be remembered.

Objective #1—Uncovering Hidden Job Opportunities

You may have heard the phrase, "There is power in numbers." The more people who are aware of your needs and skills, the better your chances are of someone knowing about a job opportunity. **That is how you uncover hidden opportunities**. People run across job openings all the time. If you tell everyone you know that you are looking, they will very likely keep you in mind if they hear of an available position that suits you. Some of your contacts may give you the name of a professional in the industry with whom you could talk. Perfect! Call that person and "tell 'em who sent ya!"

Objective #2—Increasing Your Contacts

Let's say you draft a networking list. Who would your list include? Begin with your friends, neighbors, relatives, and teachers. Take a moment to write a networking list. See how many people you can come up with in just a few minutes. For example:

Example Contact List

	NAME	CONNECTION
1.	Nick Miller	Parole Officer
2.	Lori Goldstein	Former Employer
3.	David Wells	Friend
4.	Brenda Stevens	Track Coach

Contacting Your List

When you have established your contact list, look it over. You have probably come up with a list that is larger than you expected. The important thing to remember about networking is that you don't necessarily have to be on a first-name basis with all of these people. You can list the friends of your friends, or relatives of your friends. Even if you don't know them well, include their names.

So why did you make this list? These people may be able to help you with your job search. They may know of someone who is hiring parolees, they may offer some hints on your resume, tell you more about the industry they work in, or possibly refer you to a professional they know in your field. Your objective is to set up a meeting with each contact to acquire knowledge. Contacting everyone on your list will put you one step closer to finding a job.

It's easier to network with people you know. You've probably known them for years and feel sure they would like to see you get off to a fresh start. Contact them first. Pop by their houses. Call them. Tell them that you are beginning your job search. Ask them what they think of your strategy. Most people will not be able to leave it at "Oh, I'd keep doing what you're doing." They will be compelled to give you a bit of advice!

As a matter of fact, networking is a tremendous ego booster for your contacts. It gives them a chance to show off what they know or who they know. If they feel they can help you in any way, it will make them feel helpful and useful.

Objective #3—Demonstrate Responsibility

Networking is also a way of showing employers that, despite your past, you are ready to be honest and take responsibility. You have to convince at least one employer that, if given an opportunity, you will work twice as hard as other potential employees to help their company succeed. You have to prove that you are ready to go further than the extra mile. So quit concentrating on classified ads as your sole job search tool. Remember, your time would be better spent utilizing both traditional and nontraditional job search tools.

Defusing The Bomb

When using traditional job search methods, your criminal record is likely to come up before you have a chance to convince the employer you are sincere, hard-working, reformed, and trustworthy. If the employer does not know you and becomes aware of your record before talking with you, chances are you will be "red flagged." Any job search technique that allows you to talk, meet, and win over the employer before you bring up your record is advantageous. In short, if you can meet a potential employer and convince them that you are worth taking a chance on, you are much more likely to get an offer. The employer may not have any openings themselves but they may be able to suggest other potential companies. In either case, you are better off than not getting your feet in the door at all.

Objective #4—Finding Out More Information

Informational Interviews

Suppose one of your contacts refers you to someone in the industry or you have decided to call someone in the industry on your own—someone who is doing what you would like to be doing. Now what do you do? Well, you approach your networking contact for an informational interview.

An informational interview is an invaluable aid for increasing your contacts and your awareness of the industry. Make your first contact by phone. Introduce yourself and tell your contact that you are seeking advice about your job search strategy. Explain your current situation—that you are currently unemployed (don't bring up your record at this point). Tell your contact you would like to set up a brief meeting (fifteen to twenty minutes) to get input and reactions to your resume and your career direction, and ask how they got started in the industry. The important thing to remember is that you are not calling them for a job. You don't want to put them in an awkward situation. Simply tell them you are interested in their advice and guidance and that you know, with their help, you can get on the right track!

Overcoming Reluctance

Now you are probably saying, "HOLD IT! I can't call people I barely know and start asking them for advice!" That's a normal reaction. Most people feel the same way. Until you get a few calls under your hat, you're going to feel a little nervous scheduling an informational interview. Practice scheduling the interview with a friend using note cards if needed. Keep important information close at hand. You may be surprised when you see how many people are flattered you chose to contact them.

Keeping Track

While some of the people on your list will not have the resources or time to assist you, others definitely will. Those who can help you will either set up informational interviews with you, or they will refer you to other professionals in the industry. That is where your organizational skills come in. You must keep track of your contacts, your referrals and what you have learned from each of them. Say your original contact, Ms. Brown, meets with you and then refers you to Mr. Smith—someone who knows more about the field you are interested in. The form on the **next page** will enable you to list your original contact (Ms. Brown), and then any other contact (Mr. Smith, etc.) that may stem from your original contact. This gives you a handy reference of each of your contacts and how you met them. Other helpful information to know is the date you called them, their name, position, company, phone number, and the date you arranged to meet with them. The section for Notes is to be filled in after your meeting to remind you of key points that were discussed and to help you compose a thank-you note.

For example:

> Referral List

> Original Contact:

Called: 2/19
Contact Name: Nick Miller
Position: Editor
Company: Daily Mail
Phone: 555-9543
Meeting Date: n/a

Notes: Talked to him about my job search. He referred me to Juliana Lord at Keiffer Inc. She's the Human Resources manager. She has worked on several committees with Nick Miller.

> Referred To:

Called: 2/23
Contact Name: Juliana Lord
Position: Human Resources Manager
Company: Keiffer Inc.
Phone: 555-4680
Meeting Date: 2/27 (Friday) 9:30 a.m.

Notes: Fill in after meeting.

Calling Your Contact

No matter how well you know the people on your list of contacts, calling them to network or to set up an informational interview requires you to be professional and respectful of their busy schedules. You should keep your conversations as brief as possible. Be well organized and to the point. Make it clear that you will only take a few minutes of their time. If you were referred through a contact, mention the name of the person who referred you. Here are some examples:

"Hello, Ms. Lord? My name is Edward Wilder. John Wallace suggested I contact you. I'm reentering the workforce and am very interested in pursuing a career in welding. I was wondering if I could have fifteen minutes of your time to ask you some questions. I've prepared a resume and I wondered if I could get your reaction to it and ask you a few questions about where you see the industry going in the near future."

OR

"Hello, Mr. Jones? My name is Phoebe Donovan. I'm interested in doing some data entry for the paper. I have several years of experience and wondered if I could talk to you about where you see opportunities in the area. Could we arrange a time to meet sometime next week and discuss some ideas?"

OR

"Hello, Ms. Demeuth? My name is John Fisher. I will be moving back to the Charleston area soon and am seeking a career in trucking. I have a good driving record and plenty of practical experience. I would like to talk to you about companies that might be hiring, growth in the industry and specialized careers for drivers. Could you spare fifteen or twenty minutes to meet with me?"

Of course, your conversations will not be exactly like these. Add your own personality. But the idea is still the same. Keep it organized, brief, and to the point. Some people will be difficult to contact. Don't be frustrated. Keep trying. You have plenty of people on your list and there are those who may be too busy to meet with you. Note those you have been able to reach on the form used in Exercise 4. That way, you will remember to contact them later.

Objective #5—Making Yourself Memorable

Preparing for Informational Interviews

Now that you have set up an informational interview with your contact, what are you going to talk about when sitting in their office? You promised them you would only take a few moments of their time, but you have to make sure you cover everything or the meeting will be a waste of time. You are the interviewer this time, so you will have to prepare the outline for the meeting. How will it begin, progress, and end? What questions are you going to ask? What would you like to accomplish? Once again, you will need to be organized, because the most important thing for you to do is to leave your contact with a good impression of you in case a job becomes available. Informational interviews are just as important as actual job interviews.

INTRODUCTION: If you do not know your contact very well or not at all, begin with a little information about yourself—where you are from, where you went to school, where you have worked, and why you are seeking advice. Why did you choose to interview this person at this company? Did someone refer you to her? Your introduction will familiarize your contact with your experiences and interests and provide a framework for the meeting.

GETTING TO THE POINT: You scheduled this interview so you could get your contact's advice on your job search. Whether it is advice on your resume, thoughts on where the industry is going, who is hiring, or what skills are desirable in this field, you will need to get to the point and be clear about the information you are seeking. Prepare questions ahead of time and practice them. Relate some of your questions to what you already know about the industry or your contact's company.

BRINGING UP YOUR RECORD: At some point you need to bring up your prison record. When and how you do it is up to you but do not leave it out. This act of omission would be as bad as lying. You can work it into your background or phrase it as a question. "I made a mistake and did some time for it. Do you think this will seriously hinder my chances for employment?" The most important thing to remember is to be sincere and convincing. Explain that you are not going to repeat that mistake and you will work twice as hard to prove yourself. Do not dwell on this issue. Be sure to practice this until you are very convincing. The way you handle the issue may very well make all the difference. You must win over the interviewer.

CLOSING: Before leaving, restate your goals and your enthusiasm to work in this field. Ask your contact if they know others in the industry who may be doing things differently and could give you another perspective of the field. Try to get at least two other names from your contact and keep them posted on your progress! The more people who know your name, the quicker you will be remembered the next time a job becomes available. You never know, you could impress these contacts so much that they will create a position for you!

FOLLOW UP: Always send a thank-you note to show your appreciation for the help you received during your job search—especially for an informational interview. Thank-you notes are not only courteous, but they also increase the likelihood that the employer will remember you. It is important to remember to keep these contacts in your loop. Touch base with them periodically to let them know what you are doing and that you are still out there. If they circulated your resume, find out to whom it was given. The people who have received your resume are now new contacts. Follow up with them and add them to your list. Contact them for informational interviews.

The bottom line is . . . if you network effectively, someone will remember you and possibly recommend you for the next available position. That is why it is so important to leave your contacts with a great impression of you. In the meantime, you will have made some valuable professional contacts and you will have learned useful information about the industry.

Some additional things to remember for your informational interview are:

- Arrive on time.
- Be enthusiastic, organized, and be aware of the time.
- Do not ask for a job; you are only there for advice.
- Bring extra copies of your resume. They may want to circulate it.
- Dress for success. That's how you want to be remembered.
- Do research on the company and your contact before your informational interview.
- Bring your informational interview outline (**next page**) and a pen and paper to take notes.
- Bring up your record but do not dwell on it.
- Convince the interviewer that you will work twice as hard to prove yourself.

Informational Interview Outline

How you conduct your informational interview is very important. You have a small amount of time to gather as much information as possible about your contact, the company, and the industry. By composing and following a outline, you will be sure to cover all of the bases. Practice what you will say in your informational interview. Take the outline with you to the interview. Employers like to see a candidate who is not going to waste their time, is organized, has an agenda, and follows it. You can use the following as basis for your outline:

I. INTRODUCTION
    A. Background information on myself
        1. Where I am from
        2. Education
        3. Work Experience
        4. Current Situation
    B. Reasons I am contacting this employer
        1. Referral or cold call
        2. Prison record . . . will work twice as hard
        3. Job search advice . . . other possible contacts

II. GETTING TO THE POINT
    A. I am seeking advice
        1. Resume
            a. what is his/her reaction to it
            b. suggestions
    B. I am seeking information
        1. The industry
            a. its future
            b. new innovations
            c. employment
        2. Particular field
            a. typical day
            b. responsibilities
            c. career ladder
        3. Qualifications
            a. education
            b. skills
            c. training
    C. What I know about the industry

III. CLOSING
    A. Follow through
        1. Restate your goals
        2. Show appreciation
    B. Referrals
        1. Try to get at least one referral
        2. Keep them informed of your progress

Keeping Track

Any time you have networked or have had an informational interview, you should keep track of them on your referral list. You wrote your original contact on this list. Expand your list if that contact refers you to someone else. For example:

Referral List

Called: 2/19
Contact Name: Nick Miller
Position: Editor
Company: Daily Mail
Phone: 555-9543
Meeting Date: n/a

Notes: Talked to him about my job search. He referred me to Juliana Lord at Keiffer Inc. She's the Human Resources manager. She has worked on several committees with Nick Miller.

Referred To:

Called: 2/23
Contact Name: Juliana Lord
Position: Human Resources Manager
Company: Keiffer Inc.
Phone: 555-4680
Meeting Date: 2/27 (Friday) 9:30 a.m.

Notes: She doesn't have anything right now-suggested I contact her in a few months. They plan to develop a new product and will need several people to do direct market surveys. Computer experience is helpful. She suggested I contact Bill Board at McJunkin Corporation. He is expanding their R & D department.

Referred To:

Called:
Contact Name: Bill Board
Position: Research & Development Liaison
Company: McJunkin Corporation
Phone: 555-7889
Meeting Date:

Notes: (Fill in after meeting.)

Use the following form for your personal networking schedule or as an informational interview list.

REFERRAL LIST

Called:
Contact Name:
Position:
Company:
Phone:
Meeting Date:

Notes:

REFERRED TO:

Called:
Contact Name:
Position:
Company:
Phone:
Meeting Date:

Notes:

REFERRED TO:

Called:
Contact Name:
Position:
Company:
Phone:
Meeting Date:

Notes:

The Internet

Now that just about everyone has access to a computer, and many know how to dial into on-line information services, the job search process has taken on new dimensions. Job postings, resume databases, and several job and career research resources specialize in electronically matching employers with job seekers. Ambitious individuals who know how to exploit all available resources are adding the Internet and on-line services to their proactive job search. It's a great way to stand out. Employers receiving responses to their ads on the Internet are practically guaranteed applicants who know their way around a computer. That's a plus for you—even if your computer-literate friend helped you!

The Internet has something for everyone. Job seekers can access job and career information through the expansive Internet or through specialized on-line services like America Online, CompuServe, Prodigy, or Microsoft Network, to name a few.

If you do not have access to a computer at home, most libraries now offer free access through their terminals. Ask the librarian, and while you're at it, ask if they have a career resource center.

The Internet itself is an enormous resource that includes employment-related information as well as many other topics. To find job search information, all you need is an "address" such as us.jobs.offered (not an actual address) to navigate to your destination, or you can wander through menus until you find what you need (having an address is much easier, though). Common addresses are discussed later in this chapter.

On-line services are an off-shoot of the Internet, each providing a variety of services, but all offering employment-related information. These services are easy to use and worth looking into. Some on-line services have full access to the Internet while others offer limited access. You should shop around for the on-line service that meets your needs and budget. This chapter focuses on these on-line services and how they can work for you.

Job Postings

Until recently, the vast majority of jobs listed on-line have been technically oriented. Now, you can find listings for just about everything as companies are drawn by the relatively low cost of listing openings on-line. Each on-line service has a different niche. Some maintain a database largely for white-collar jobs while others concentrate on specific companies ranging from AT&T to small consulting firms.

Job postings can be searched by industry, occupation, location, or a combination of these. Depending on the on-line service, some charge a fee to the person placing the ad, others charge the job-seeker who searches the listings, yet most are FREE!

View quickly . . .

Users should be aware of the associated costs of using on-line services such as long-distance phone charges or per hour charges. Until you can navigate quickly through these services, keep an eye on how long you are on the Internet; otherwise, you may end up with a bill you can ill afford. Time is definitely money. On-line charges vary from service to service and often change. Most on-line services charge a monthly fee, say $10.95, and then an hourly fee after your first five, or so, hours. On-line services at your school, state employment office, or library may be free and a good place to start. Check into those first—until you know your way around. Many services offer a flat-fee, unlimited use option. Outside of free connections via the library, this may be your best option when using on-line services and the Internet for your job search.

. . . and frequently

Listings change frequently on the Internet as it may be costly for an employer to pay for an out dated advertisement. Check the listings regularly and respond immediately, and not just for one service. Investigate several. Finding a job is a numbers game. The more contacts you make, the better your chances of finding a job. You can easily respond to ads by mail, phone, fax, or on-line.

Resume Databases

Resume databases are on the rise with the computer's ability to handle massive amounts of information, and its ability to scan for specific information such as experience, skills, geographic preference, degree, and other qualifications.

Depending on the on-line service, resumes can be uploaded or E-mailed directly into the system; filled out on-line; or faxed to the service where they will be scanned or entered manually by the service's staff.

Again, cost is a factor. These services charge either the employer per search or the candidate identified by the search. However, if you look at the costs of sending thousands of resumes through the postal service, you will see the Internet can help you reach more people with substantially less cost.

Your resume can be viewed directly by a potential employer or searched by the staff of the database service. One thing to note: once your resume is put onto the system, it may be stripped of any fancy fonts and bold or italicized type. You will need to rely on spacing and upper and lower case type to make your resume stand out.

Your resume could be scanned for specific information. For example, a resume can be scanned to search for nouns such as accountant, clerk, librarian, manager, or editor, or it can be scanned to look for verbs such as promoted, increased, improved, organized, or decreased. The best services will help you tailor your resume, qualifications, skills, and experience to the form their computer search recognizes.

Best of Both Worlds

If you search further, you'll find that a number of on-line services offer both job listings and a resume database—and that's not all. Many services also include useful material for your overall job search including: networking opportunities, interviewing suggestions, and weekly discussion groups.

Do the Services Really Work?

Although it's hard to tell how many candidates actually land a job through the Internet, it's a fact that the more miles logged on these services, the better the odds of finding a job. Being the largest word-of-mouth resource in the world, the networking opportunities on the Internet are limitless! Nowhere else can you economically chat with thousands of people about your job search and interests. So, do they really work? Well, it is interesting to note that companies both large and small are subscribing to these on-line recruiting methods at a steady rate. And as employment experts will verify, searching for and landing a job requires a multifaceted, proactive approach-which means utilizing every job search tool available to you.

Why the Internet for the Ex-Offender?

The Internet can be an invaluable resource for the ex-offender in search of a job. Using the Internet and on-line services to network allows you to inexpensively expand the geographical area of your job search from your local area to the nation . . . indeed, to the world! If the geographical area you are currently covering does not have many employers willing to hire ex-offenders, the Internet allows you to cover a great deal more. If the area you are in has a high unemployment rate, the Internet allows you to search in areas where unemployment is lower, demand for employees is higher, or openings for jobs with specialized skills you may have developed is greater. Be sure to check with your parole officer about restrictions on moving.

Major Companies

Most major corporations and many smaller companies are listing available job openings on their web sites. They are particularly likely to list openings for which there is a scarcity of qualified applicants. If you have skills specific to a particular industry, trade group, or union, go to web sites specific to those organizations and look for positions.

Major On-Line Services

All major on-line services offer some sort of job- and career-related information. Pick the service that meets your needs and your budget. Many software packages include free introductory time on their service. Take advantage of this opportunity to explore what they have to offer.

America Online (AOL)

America Online Inc.
8619 Westwood Center Drive
Vienna, VA 22182-2285
800-827-6364
703-448-8700

America Online's Careers Board offers a variety of job search and career information including: employer contacts, job listings, resume and cover letter databases, and more.

CompuServe

CompuServe Inc.
5000 Arlington Centre Boulevard
P.O. Box 20212
Columbus, OH 43220
800-848-8199

CompuServe, a predominantly business-oriented on-line service, offers job search listings and bulletin boards covering subjects such as law, marketing, aviation, broadcasting, and others. This service also includes an extensive number of newspapers, periodicals, and other research material to aid your job search.

Prodigy

Prodigy Services Company
445 Hamilton Avenue
White Plains, NY 10601
800-776-3449

Prodigy, an easy-to-use service, offers job listings, reference material, and a Careers Bulletin Board for networking with other professionals.

Delphi

A Service of General Videotex Corporation
1038 Massachusetts Avenue
Cambridge, MA 02138
800-695-4005
617-491-6642

Delphi offers job listings, interview exercises, and an Internet gopher that has the ability to search for any subject matter including job- and career-related material.

GEnie

General Electric Network for Information Exchange
401 North Washington Street
Rockville, MD 20850
800-638-9636

GEnie offers a variety of job search information including Dr. Job, a weekly question and answer column offering career and employment advice. It also offers E-Span Job Search listings, a Peer-to-Peer Network for specialized industry discussions found in a Health Care Providers Category, a Judge & Lawyer's
Category, an Engineer's Category, and more.

Useful Internet Addresses

The easiest way to get anywhere is to have an address. The same theory applies to the Internet. Sure, you can wander around until you find what you are looking for, like you might find a friend's house, but the Internet contains a variety of employment-related newsgroups, or articles, that can give you advice or help you find employment anywhere in the world. Several useful newsgroups are listed below.

Adams Jobbank Online
http://www.adamsjobbank.com
> Thousands of job openings worldwide with search engine and job search information

AT&T College Network
http://www.att.com/college
> Job listings, job links, advice

America's Job Bank
http://www.ajb.dni.us/index.html
> Huge database of job opportunities

Business-To-Business Marketing Exchange
http://www.mba.wfu.edu/b2b.html
> Jobs in marketing field

Career Magazine
http://www.careermag.com/careermag
> Job opportunities, resume bank, career section

Career Mosaic
http://www.careermosaic.com
> Jobs, career resources, resume posting

Careerpath
http://www.careerpath.com
> Scan employment listings from largest newspapers

Careerweb
http://www.cweb.com
> Job listings, search, job matching system

College Grad Job Hunter
http://www.collegegrad.com
> Entry-level jobs for college graduates with job search tips

Direct Marketing World's Job Center
http://www.dmworld.com
> Professional job openings in direct marketing industry

Employment Edge
http://sensemedia.net/employment.edge
> Employment database, job search info, salary info, resume posting

Entry Level Job Seeker Assistant
http://www.utsi.edu:70/students
> For persons who have never held a full time job

Federal Jobs Central
http://www.fedjobs.com
> Fee site offering subscription to publication with 3,500 plus federal job openings

Federal Jobs Digest
http://www.jobsfed.com
> Wide range of federal job openings

Fedworld
http://www.fedworld.gov
> Over 3,000 federal job openings by state

Fleet House Career Match
http://www.fleethouse.com/career
> Pay service (low cost) to match job seekers and employers, post resumes

4Work
http://www.4work.com
> Employment opportunities at fortune 500 companies, search engine

Help Wanted - USA
http://www.webcom.com/~career/hwusa.html
> Resume bank and job listings with search engine

Intellimatch
http://www.intellimatch.com
> Resume posting with job matching system

Job Web
http://www.jobweb.com
> Sophisticated job matching search, internships, federal jobs, career planning

Marketing Classifieds on the Internet

http://www.marketingjobs.com

Nationwide marketing, sales and advertising jobs, resume posting

Medsearch America

http://www.medsearch.com

Large site listing medically related jobs nationwide with search engine and resume posting

The Monster Board

http://www.monster.com

Over 60,000 job listings nationwide with career search, employer profiles-huge site!

National Multimedia Association of America's JOB BANKER

http://www.nmaa.org/jobbank.html

Good search engine for matching employers and employees

Online Career Center

http://www.occ.com

Listings from over 30 U.S. corporations, resume posting, job fairs-great site

StudentCenter

http://www.studentcenter.com

Allows user to browse over 40,000 companies & 1,000 industries-career info, job search tips, resume posting

Virtual Job Fair

http://www.vjf.com

Job search, resume center, career information, more

Zdnet Job Database

http://www/zdnet.com/~zdi/jobs/jobs.html

U.S. job search directory with search engine

Chapter 7

Trying the Traditional Approach

Answering Classified Ads

Ask job hunters how to quickly and easily find a job, and many will tell you to read the classified help-wanted ads published in your local newspaper. It sounds simple. Just pick the ads that interest you, and place your cover letter and resume into an envelope, and drop it into the mail box. Then go home and wait for the phone to ring. It could be a long wait. Remember, many employers don't place an ad in the paper. If you only read the newspaper, you'll miss out on most job opportunities. This is only one of the ways you should be looking for a job.

Blind Ads Can Be Dangerous To Your Career

A large percentage of help-wanted ads are signed with a box number. The job sounds great, and you are anxious to get your resume in the mail. But wait! You have no idea who the advertiser is.

Why do firms use box numbers instead of their names? They may not want competitors to know they are hiring. Personnel departments may want to avoid the hassle of handling the large number of telephone calls that could result from a signed advertisement.

Should you bypass blind ads completely? Not necessarily, but you should be skeptical. Remember that when you respond to a blind ad, you are telling strangers your name, address, telephone number, and complete personal and employment history.

Here are a few general questions to ask yourself when answering help-wanted classified advertising:
- Does the ad describe what the company does?
- Does it manufacture a product, perform a service, or sell information? Does the job even sound appealing to you?
- Does it specify how much experience and what kind of education or training are required?
- Does it show the title of the job?
- Does the ad specify a salary range?

Why the Newspaper is a Good Source

Don't forget the primary reason for the newspaper is because of its news! Read the paper every day. Look for articles that are talking about new companies that are coming to your area. That company just may be hiring for a position that interests you. Call the company directly and ask them if they have any openings.

Career Services

Career counselors are everywhere and many are very helpful. They are called career consultants, job counselors, vocational guidance counselors, industrial psychologists, and career development specialists. Some career counselors specialize in helping ex-offenders find a job.

Here are some of the things they may do for you:

√ Help you prepare a cover letter and a resume.
√ Administer tests to determine your skills.
√ Analyze your career goals.
√ Videotape practice interview sessions to help you deal with the incarceration issue.
√ Circulate your resume to a list of companies who may or may not have job openings.

If your case worker can't help you find a career center to help you with your job search, look in the business and help wanted sections of newspapers. Be sure to ask about and be prepared to pay the fees private career counselors charge. Remember, many of these services are offered free at your YMCA/YWCA, one stop career center, or job service office.

How to Find the Good Guys

Explore the nonprofit organizations. Educational institutions (colleges, universities, community colleges, and some high schools) employ vocational counselors with the appropriate educational and professional qualifications. Professional societies and trade associations often provide career guidance services, as do some government agencies such as the State Employment Service and the Veterans Administration. Check with all these sources. The length and scope of programs vary widely and you can choose the one that fits your needs.

To locate professional career counselors in your area, contact The National Board for Certified Counselors (NBCC). They are located at 3-D Terrace Way, Greensboro, NC 27403. They publish a list of career counselors who have been certified.

Here are some things that board certified career counselors do:

- Conduct personal counseling sessions with individuals and groups to help clarify career goals and interests and identify career options.
- Provide opportunities for improving decision-making skills.
- Teach job hunting strategies and skills and assist in the development of resumes.
- Help resolve potential personal conflicts on the job through practice in human relations skills.
- Provide support for persons experiencing job stress, job loss, and career transition.

Whether you seek help from commercial counseling firms, certified professionals, or nonprofit organizations, make sure you understand the service, what you have to do, and what costs are involved.

Chapter 8

Putting It On Paper

Now that you have an idea of what you may like to do, and who may help you, your credentials need to be put in writing. This can be in the form of a general letter, an application, or a resume.

A general letter or resume is written and mailed to a prospective employer. You will describe your skills, experience, education and employment goals. Your goal is to convince the employer to meet with you for an interview. Therefore, it is important that you do the best you can in creating this material. In fact, get some help in writing them. Your caseworker or release counselor should be able to help you. Other sources of assistance are your local Job Service Office or Career Service Center.

The application is something you normally fill out on the spot while you are in the employer's office. It will ask you where you went to school, how many years of education you received, where and for how long you have worked and what you expect to be paid. The application may also include a place for you to list your references and their phone numbers, and maybe write a paragraph of why you want this job.

It is hard to fill out an application when you don't have the dates you have worked or your references memorized. **Here is a hint: write this information down and keep it with you.** When you are handed the application, pull out your list and begin writing. Employers use this information to choose who they will interview for the job.

What About THE Question?

If there is a question about your criminal record, simply state "Yes, I have a record Let's discuss it in the interview." Then, be ready to talk about it. A face-to-face encounter will give you more opportunity to talk about your past without automatically being turned down. You will be held accountable for everything you put on your application. Think about how you will handle this question before going in an office to fill one out. The application will probably ask that you explain your answer. Don't go into detail. Again, wait for the interview.

What if you just say "no" to that question? You could be caught after they investigate your past, which would result in being fired. It is simply not worth it to always have that bomb ticking away. Better to build your new life on a record of honesty, truthfulness, and hard work. Put it on the table, deal with it, and then put it behind you. Having that act of omission hanging over your head ready to explode and mess up your life again is no way to live.

APPLICATIONS

When filling out an application, remember it is as important as a resume. When the employer looks at an application, it should be complete and clearly written. Have a list of all the information you will need with you: your address and phone number as well as those for your former employers, and the dates you worked. If you do not have a phone, give the phone number of a friend or relative who has agreed to take messages for you.

Before you begin filling out the application, read it carefully. Make sure you understand all the questions and can see how much space you have available to write your answers. Be sure to answer every question as best you can and follow all instructions. If it says to "print" in ink, then use a pen and print.

Create a Master Form

Sometimes you are given an application to take home and fill out. This will give you extra time to think about what you are writing. Ask if you may have an extra copy. You can practice on one copy and then neatly fill out the copy you will be submitting. Type or print neatly in blue or black ink. Check your spelling. And sign and date the application before delivering it.

The practice copy can be used as a guide in the future when you fill out more applications. You will find that most applications ask the same questions. This may get boring, but keep in mind a different person will review each application. Also, neatness counts. Employers do not want to decipher your handwriting when looking at your application.

RESUMES

Resumes are nothing to be afraid of. You are simply telling someone else what you want them to know about you. Many jobs may not require a resume, but it makes a good impression if you have one. It makes an even better impression if your resume looks good. A resume is just a piece of paper containing information about you: where you live, your phone number, where you received your training or went to school, where you've worked, and what types of skills you have learned in the last 5 to 10 years.

For example, if you want to prepare food, then your resume should reflect any food preparation experience you have had, where you worked, and for how long. Employers hold your resume up to the requirements of their available job to decide if they have a match.

If you don't know what you want to do, prepare a simple, general resume. A general resume lists all the information from above, but it is not targeted to a particular job.

You Only Get a Few Seconds

Resumes don't get read—they get scanned. About 15 seconds worth. It is called "screening," and is usually done by personnel assistants or clerks who, faced with a stack of resumes up to their chins, have developed what they call the 3-stack system.

During the 15 second glance, the reader decides whether the resume should go into one of three stacks, marked "YES", "NO", or "MAYBE." The "YES" resumes go up to the next level for another screening. The "NOs" go in the trash, and the "MAYBEs" just lay there for a few days, after which they usually follow the "NOs."

Here are some of the ways to make sure your resume gets to the right stack every time.

Write the Right Resume

There are many ways to write a resume. One good way is to organize your resume by the skills and experience you have. This resume format is called a functional resume. It is a good format for those who have gaps in their employment, who have changed jobs often, or who have a period of time during which they were incarcerated. Instead of giving the names and dates you worked, list the job you held and the length of time you were there. Your references and places of employment can be available upon request. **See the example on the next page.**

The Long and Short of It

How long should a resume be? One page, if possible, but never more than two pages. For applicants looking for their first jobs or having one or two years of experience, a single-page resume is sufficient. Since your background is limited, there isn't much to say, and one page contains more than enough space to say it.

For those with several years of experience, a second page may be used—but stop there. If you need more space, you are probably trying to say too much, or you are using too many words to say it. Again, find someone to help you write your resume. They will help you make your resume the right length and to say what is needed.

Your Record and Your Resume

You should not include your record on your resume. It is simply not part of your work record and it is not the appropriate time to bring it up. Remember, the main purpose of a resume is to get an interview. During the interview you can employ maximum damage control and minimize the adverse effects of your record. You may even be able to convince the interviewer that you are fully prepared to work harder and longer than others to prove yourself. If you mention your record on the resume, you may never get a chance to explain and convince.

John Fischer
111 Main Street
Charleston, N.C. 46383
(304) 555-2000

EMPLOYMENT GOAL: Short Order Cook

EXPERIENCE:

- One-year, short order cook, prepared food cooked to order such as hamburgers, hot dogs, eggs, bacon, toast, sandwiches.
- One-year, part-time at Hardee's restaurant, in charge of grills, deep-fryer, soft-serve ice cream machine.
- Two-years, full-time cook at Pam's Homemade Pizza. Everything was made from scratch.
- One year, part-time cleaning service for industrial size kitchen. Sanitized counters, sinks and utensils. Mopped floors and took out daily garbage.
- One summer, bus person. Cleaned and set tables. Served water, coffee and tea to customers.

EDUCATION:

- 11th grade education. Mostly "B" average at Benton High School, Benton, N.C.
- G.E.D. with honors, average of 60.
- On-the-job training

REFERENCES:

References and places of employment available upon request.

Include the Following Items on Your Resume.

Identification: Put your name, address and telephone number where you can be reached at the top of your resume.

Objective or Employment Goal: State an example of what you would like to do such as "Short Order Cook." Or, state a few general examples if you aren't sure what you would like to do.

Work Experience: List every job you have held in the last five to ten years, starting with the most recent one and working backwards. Briefly describe the duties you held in each job. Include any equipment you operated. Mention if you worked with the public or with customers.

Education: List your education, including high school, technical school, community school, or any courses or training you may have taken. Don't list the dates you attended, if you do not want to emphasize the breaks in your educational history. Make sure you add the G.E.D. if you completed that.

Military Experience: Military experience looks good on anyone's resume. List the dates of service and the branch. If related to the job you are applying for, list the duties you performed while in the service.

References. References are lists of people who will say you either worked for them or people who can say you are a good worker. Think of two or three people to list as your references. At the bottom of your resume, write "References are available upon request." The information you will need is your references' full names, job titles, addresses, and phone numbers. Make sure you ask your references if they mind you listing them. Keep your list of references handy in case you are asked for it.

6 Resume Tips

1. Be neat. A sloppy resume indicates a sloppy applicant.
2. Be honest, but don't include anything negative on your resume. Be ready to explain anything negative if it comes up in the interview, such as your record.
3. Don't list personal information such as age, weight, height or marital status.
4. Make sure your grammar is correct. Have someone check for spelling and punctuation.
5. Never include the following on your resume:
   - Religion or church affiliation
   - Race, color, or national origin
   - Political preferences
   - Previous or anticipated salary information
   - Reasons for leaving previous positions
   - Opinions of former employers
   - Hobbies

6. Use a good typewriter or word processor and use a high quality bond paper.

Think Before You Write

Think about what you would like to say on your resume. Use the following as a guide.

Identification

- Your full name

    _____

- Your complete address

    _____

    _____

    _____

- Home telephone number or number where you can get messages

    _____

- Your objective or title of position for which you are applying

    _____

- Your education

    - Name and location of high school or place where you received your G.E.D.

        _____

    - Name and location of college, if you attended

        _____

        _____

    - Dates attended

        _____

    - Diploma or degree received, including major course of study

        _____

• Other education: technical schools, company training, seminars, apprenticeships

_____

_____

_____

• Special school honors, extracurricular activities, academic societies, or special study groups

_____

_____

_____

• Cooperative school/work programs, internships, or certificates

_____

_____

• Your title and experience for each job

_____

_____

_____

_____

_____

_____

• Name and address of employer for 1st job

_____

_____

_____

• Name and address of employer for 2nd job

_____

_____

_____

• Name and address of employer for 3rd job

_____

_____

_____

• Name and address of employer for 4th job

_____

_____

_____

• Accomplishments — be specific. For each job, include what you did to improve your job, save time, increase sales, save money, etc.

_____

_____

_____

_____

• Promotions and special awards

_____

_____

• Computer programs, languages, and technical ability

_____

_____

• Membership in business organizations, trade groups, and professional societies

_____

_____

_____

Final Checklist

You have completed your resume. You can't imagine how an employer can resist it. Before you mail it to someone, check it out.

- Is your address and telephone number accurate?
- Did you include all of your education and experience?
- Is the grammar correct?
- Are there any misspelled words?
- Is the copy clean and sharp?
- Have you capitalized your headings?
- Is it printed or copied on high-quality paper?

Chapter 9

The Cover Letter

Are cover letters important? Are they even necessary? For some jobs, you can bet on it!

Once you have completed your resume and have found the jobs you would like to apply for, prepare a cover letter to introduce yourself to the employer and ask for an interview.   Of two hundred employers recently surveyed, seventy-two percent said that they considered the cover letter to be an essential part of a candidate's job application. Of course, that depends on the job.

What is a cover letter and what does it accomplish? First and foremost, it is a sales letter. Its purpose is to persuade a prospective employer that your background and experience shown on your resume makes you a great person for the job. If you have specialized skills that are in demand, this is a good time and place to emphasize them.

Too many job applicants don't realize the importance of the cover letter. Here are a few examples of what NOT to do:

Box T3458
New York Times
New York, NY 10108

Dear Sir:

Here is my resume. When may we meet?

Sincerely yours,
David Roth

Mr. Tom Lester
Director of Human Resources
Mainstream Publishing Co.
485 Market Street
Philadelphia, PA. 19154

Dear Mr. Lester:

A resume is attached.

Yours truly,
Joan Reilly

Longacre Employment Agency
17 West 46th Street
New York, NY 10036

Gentlemen:

In response to your ad in the New York Post, I
am looking for work that can be done in
Manhattan.

Sincerely,
Ian Rich

Let's look at the positive points of these letters. . . OK, there aren't any. **These are examples of what NOT to do.**

A useful cover letter should be simple, short, and to-the-point. Address your letter to a specific person and list their title. If you don't know the person's name, call the company and ask to whom your letter should be addressed. If this is a classified ad you are answering, mention the ad. If someone you know referred you to this job or told you to speak to this person, mention your referral's name—with your referral's approval, of course.

In your cover letter, describe your skills and abilities, especially those that fit the requirements of the job. Close the letter by asking for an interview. Make sure your telephone number, with the area code, is written somewhere on the letter. **See the example on the following page.**

Fred Mays
121 Maple Drive
Wallbash, MI 55823
(402) 555-2555

January 22, 2020

Mr. John Edwards
Manager
Edwards Landscaping Company
200 Elk Street
Wallbash, MI 55825

Dear Mr. Edwards,

I am answering your ad for a landscaping assistant in today's *Wallbash News*. Because of my work experience, I believe I can do the job well.

I have two years experience working in the landscaping business and have planted trees, flowers and prepared soil. I enjoy working outside and think I was born with a green thumb. I am hard-working and reliable.

Enclosed is my resume. I am eager to meet with you to discuss my qualifications further. I will contact you shortly to ensure that you have received my resume. Until then, I can be reached at the number above if you have any questions.

Sincerely,

Fred Mays

Letter Perfect

Believe it or not, with all the availability of electronic typewriters, word processors, and computers, people still send handwritten cover letters. Some can't even be read because of poor handwriting.

Type or have your letter printed on a good quality paper. Don't write your cover letter on a yellow legal sheet, memo, newsprint, or some other type of paper. Write a new cover letter for every job. Don't photocopy your cover letter and reuse it. Prepare a new cover letter for each job you apply for so that you can give details of your qualifications for that job.

Things to Remember - DOs and DON'Ts

DO address your letter to an individual. Use his or her correct title and be sure the name is spelled correctly.

DO describe duties and responsibilities that you have accomplished in the past.

DO mention special skills you have learned (e.g. welding, software packages you have mastered, etc.)

DO use simple words and short sentences to get your message across quickly and clearly.

DO mention that you are a fast learner if you think you lack some of the qualifications for a particular job.

DO check your letter carefully before mailing for spelling, punctuation, grammar, and sentence structure.

DO have another person read your letter. A fresh viewpoint can be very helpful.

DO keep a copy of every letter you send.

DO mail a second cover letter and another copy of your resume if you don't receive a response in two weeks. Resumes are sometimes lost, misplaced, or buried.

DON'T give reasons for anything suspicious on your resume, such as lapses in employment. Save this discussion for the interview.

DON'T discuss salary. Salary discussions belong in the interview. Stating past earnings or making salary demands before you know all the details of a job is not a good idea.

DON'T bad-mouth previous employers. Any criticism makes employers nervous. Your ex-boss may have been the biggest jerk in the industry, but don't spread it around. It could backfire. A prospective employer is apt to consider your grievances "sour grapes," making him wonder if he will eventually get the same treatment.

DON'T set conditions and make demands regarding travel, relocation, expense accounts, or education. Questions about health insurance and other benefits should be raised only when you are close to being offered a position.

DON'T list references in a cover letter. You don't want to take the chance of references being contacted until you know more about the company and the job.

DON'T give your age in a cover letter.

DON'T volunteer information about yourself that has no relevance to your qualifications. Too much information can keep you from getting the job.

DON'T exaggerate. You may be considered overqualified.

Follow Up Your Mailing

Most job applicants send resumes, answer ads, register with employment agencies, and network — ONLY ONCE — then wonder why the phone doesn't ring and the offers don't roll in. Often, it is the follow-up that gets you the job. Calling strangers may make you nervous. But, do you want the job? Do you need a job? It's worth it. The extra effort makes you stand out and you need that in your corner right now.

Three to five days after you mail your resume and cover letter, call the individual to whom you addressed your letter. If a secretary picks up the telephone, you may hit a stone wall in getting through. It is part of a secretary's job to screen incoming calls. Once you get through to the right party, start the conversation by being positive.

• "Hello Ms. Cooper. This is Frank Robinson. I hope you've had a chance to read the letter and material I sent you on March 15th." (Don't hesitate and wait for a response. Keep talking.)

• "As I mentioned in my letter, I have a lot of experience as a short order cook, and I am interested in talking to you about working for your restaurant. Could we arrange an interview to discuss this further? Say, Thursday at 10:00?"

So far, you have not actually asked for a job, but you have made your listener aware that you sent a letter and a resume. You have also reminded him or her of an important aspect of your background.

If the response to your speech is completely negative, and you are told, in so many words to "buzz off," don't get upset. Go on to the next call immediately. You won't connect on every contact, but if you continue to send out letters and follow up each prospect, you should get interviews.

If you are not successful in reaching the person to whom you sent your resume, mail another copy. There is a chance that he or she never saw the first copy. It may have been delegated to a subordinate. If, after another call or two, you continue to get nowhere, take the hint, and go on to the next prospect.

Chapter 10

The Job Interview

If you are thinking of skipping the interview, forget it. The person considering hiring you will want to meet you and ask a few questions about you and your qualifications. You need to present yourself in the best possible way. You have to be on time, look presentable and be ready to talk about yourself.

Bring your resume and completed application to the interview. Also bring your Social Security Card or green card and proof of your education or training. It is a good idea to have these things on hand.

The trick to all interviews is to win the support, enthusiasm, and trust of the interviewer. There are few situations more "artificial" than an interview. The interviewer is trying to size up the interviewee. "Is this the best possible person to fill this opening at the salary this job will pay?" You must convince the interviewer that you have the ability, attitude, and willingness to do a great job. You have to convince them that you are well aware that your record is a major negative but that you are <u>so</u> determined to prove yourself, <u>so</u> motivated to do a good job, and <u>so</u> dependable that they should give you a chance. You should not beg but you should be very sincere. Show dignity, determination, and sincerity in your approach and appearance. You may experience a great deal of rejection but it only takes <u>one</u> success. An interview is easier if you have an idea of what to expect.

Tests

You may be asked to take any number of tests as part of the interview process. They could ask you to take a skills test, such as typing or running a machine. They could ask you to take a drug test, a physical test, or even a test that will assess your personality. Be prepared for any or all of these. If you expect them, you will do better on them. The interviewer is trying to make sure you are who you say you are and that you can do what you say you can do.

How's Your Image?

Image is about the only thing you have to sell for the first five minutes of your interview. Make it a good one. Cleanliness is more important than the clothes you wear. If you can't afford new clothes, you may want to shop in a used clothing store or borrow an outfit from a friend. Dress to impress, but don't overdo it. Wear clothing that would seem right for the job.

Pick a conservative look if you aren't sure what would be best: dark colors such as blue and brown are usually best. Wear a white long sleeve shirt and polished shoes. Men should not wear noticeable jewelry and women should keep their jewelry small and to a minimum.

Don't wear strong aftershave or perfume. The smell can really be distracting. By all means, wear deodorant.

Pay special attention to your hair, teeth, and nails. Do they look presentable? You would be surprised how quickly people will judge you based on how you look. If you want the cards stacked in your favor, pay special attention to your entire look. You want it to be neat, clean, and sharp.

Stay Calm

The best preparation you can do for your interview is learn how to relax. Nearly everyone gets a little nervous before an interview. Know exactly how you are going to deal with your record. If you know what your plan of action is, you will handle yourself much better. Know what types of questions you want to ask. Rehearse the interview in your mind. Better yet, rehearse the interview with a friend or relative. Do it over and over and over ... until you are satisfied. The more planning you do before the interview, the easier it will be.

Remember, this one interview is not the end or the beginning of the world. Look at it as a learning experience and do your best. Everything you learn from this interview will help you with the next one.

Go Prepared

Learn something about the company before going for an interview. Know what the company does and the type of people they work with. Go to the library and get newspaper stories about the company, annual reports, and anything else that would be helpful. Ask the librarian for advice and assistance.

Part of giving a good impression is arriving early—about ten minutes. Make sure you know how to get to your interview so you aren't late. Make arrangements for transportation if you don't have a car. Use the extra ten minutes to think about what you want to accomplish in the interview.

When you are waiting for your appointment, take care not to slouch and fidget in the waiting room. Do not chew gum. The receptionist might be taking note of everything you do. You don't want him or her reporting anything negative about your behavior to the interviewer.

Be courteous to everyone you meet. Be organized and prepared. You may have to fill out an application form if you didn't before. Don't refuse to just because you have a resume with you. The employer needs an application from everyone. Bring a pen and paper, as well as a few copies of your resume, a list of references , and any questions you want to ask about the job. You will be more confident having these with you.

Be Positive

No matter what the topic, phrase your answer in the most positive way you can. You never want to seem argumentative or negative. If you are talking about your record, accept responsibility for your actions and express how sorry you are for what happened. Express how your past has prompted you to turn your life around and make improvements.

Don't talk badly about former employers or former experiences. You need to be in a positive frame of mind about everything you discuss in the interview. Remember, employers want employees who possess a good attitude—a can-do attitude. For example, he or she will ask you questions such as:

- How did you hear about this job?
- What kind of training or experience do you have?
- Describe your prior work experiences and responsibilities.
- How do you think you can contribute to my company?
- What do you know about my company?
- Why do you want to work for me?
- Why have you had so many jobs?
- What are your strengths?
- What are your weaknesses?
- Why did you leave your last job? (This may be the right time to explain your conviction.)
- What have you learned from your mistakes?
- Are you willing to undergo periodic drug tests?
- Why should I hire you?
- What salary do you expect?

What Questions Will You Ask?

Once you have answered the employer's questions, ask some of your own. Prepare a list of questions before the interview and bring them with you. Examples of these questions are:

- What will a typical day on the job be like for me?
- Why did the last person leave this position?
- What are the work hours? Is there a schedule?
- Are there advancement opportunities?
- Are there training opportunities?
- What are you looking for in the person you are hiring?
- How is my performance evaluated?
- Is there travel involved in this position?

Those are just a sample. You can find more questions at the library or at a career service center. Sometimes, if you imagine what the employer is looking for in an employee, you can anticipate what the questions might be.

The best way to prepare for an interview is to practice answering questions with a friend, relative, or counselor. The more you practice, the easier the actual interview will be.

15 Ways To Tame An Interviewer

1. Speak clearly.
2. Use the interviewer's name frequently during the session: Mrs. Smith, Mr. Jones.
3. Offer your hand when entering the office and give a firm handshake.
4. Smile frequently but not continuously.
5. Show enthusiasm. Attitude can often carry more weight than qualifications. Companies don't need any more employees who consider their jobs as places to go between lunch and coffee breaks.
6. Act as if you are really happy to be interviewed, even though you would rather be somewhere else. Your interviewer might also rather be elsewhere.
7. If offered an employment application before the interview, do not refuse to fill it out because you already have a resume.
8. Don't smoke.
9. Do not get personal with your interviewer. Restrict your questions and answers to those concerning the job.
10. Maintain direct eye contact. Shifty eyes convey a shifty character.
11. Get across to your interviewer that you work well under pressure. Meeting deadlines is a top priority in modern business.
12. Don't knock former employers. If you can't say something nice, don't say anything.
13. Never beg for a job. It is self-destructive.
14. Project a good image. Your image is formed by your appearance, your speech, and your attitude. You will never get a second chance to make a good first impression.
15. Be honest.

30 Ways To Self-Destruct

These practices will almost ensure that you will NOT get the job:

1. Arrive late with one of the following excuses:
    "The battery on my watch died."
    "My contact lens fell into my cereal and I couldn't find it."
    "I couldn't locate the building."
    "I took the wrong bus (subway, highway, turn)."
    "I didn't realize you were in this part of town."
    "I forgot my resume and had to go back home for it."
    "The zipper on my pants broke and I couldn't find another pair."

2. Offer a handful of rubbery fingers giving the interviewer the impression that he or she has gotten hold of a dead octopus. Or, squeeze the hand tightly until he begs for mercy.

3. Ask for an ash tray and light up a cigarette.

4. When asked why you are looking for another job, say that your last employer was a jerk who didn't know which side was up.

5. Chew gum.

6. Make yourself comfortable. Slouch back in your seat and extend your legs under the interviewer's desk.

7. Start off by asking about benefits: salary, health and retirement benefits.

8. When the interviewer asks what you know about his company, tell him you haven't the foggiest idea.

9. Say your record was the result of a frame up. You were not at fault.

10. When asked the name of your present employer, say "It's confidential."

11. Interrupt the interviewer frequently to make your points.

12. When asked for a resume tell the interviewer one of the following:
    "The dog ate my resume."
    "I don't believe in resumes."
    "I forgot it at home and will mail it."
    "My cat mistook it for the litter box."
    "I haven't had time to update it."

13. Wear strong perfume or cologne.

14. Wear blue jeans to the interview.

15. Be a name dropper.

16. Ask for assurance that the company is in good financial shape.

17. Explain the fact that you held six jobs in eight years by saying that none of them offered you enough of a challenge.

18. When asked why you are looking for a job, explain that you are two months overdue on your car payments, or that your unemployment insurance is about to expire.

20. Tell jokes.

21. Address the interviewer immediately by his or her first name.

22. Monopolize the conversation. Don't let the interviewer get a word in edgewise.

23. Wear lots of jewelry.

24. When asked about your goals, tell the interviewer that you want to learn as much as possible so that you can go into business for yourself.

25. If the interviewer should say, "Tell me about yourself," review your entire life starting when you graduated kindergarten. Don't stop talking until his or her eyes glaze over.

26. Name an outrageous salary expectation.

27. Mention that you are unwilling to travel and you would definitely not want to relocate under any circumstances.

28. Answer the question, "Why did you leave your last position" by stating "I couldn't get along with my boss."

29. When asked what your immediate goal is, tell the interviewer that you would like to have his job.

30. Avoid eye contact at all costs.

The Interview Structure

Some interviews last 15 minutes, others last all day. The length of your interview will depend on the company, the interviewer, and the job. If the job carries a lot of responsibility, they will want to thoroughly interview you. Your interview could be on the shorter side, with one interviewer.

Your meeting may go something like this: you will meet in an office, shake hands, and then make small talk for a few minutes. This is where you get to make your first impression.

Greet the interviewer by his or her name, offer a firm handshake, and then wait to be asked to be seated.

After you discuss the weather or other small topics, the interviewer will change the pace of your meeting. This is where you'll get to the heart of the meeting and discuss the job and the company, and what skills and abilities you have to offer them.

Be specific when answering the interviewer's questions. Don't talk so long that you get off the subject. The interviewer will be eager to learn a lot about you, but don't take that to mean that he or she wants to hear your personal problems. The interview is not the place to talk about what is going on in your personal life. Simply tell the interviewer your capabilities for doing the job that is available.

That Dreaded Question

"I see you left the question about any felony convictions blank on your application. Was this an oversight?" There you have it. *The* question. The question you have been afraid of since you started looking for a job.

The only solution is to be prepared to deal with your criminal record honestly and up front.

And you may not have a choice. Many parole and probation departments require under law that you disclose your past when interviewing for a job. Decide how you will answer this question *before* you go into the interview. Many ex-offenders begin their job search by telling the truth about their record. However, once they've been rejected for the 20th time, they decide "honesty perhaps isn't the best policy." But, if you decide to cover it up, you will run the risk of getting caught. And if you are caught, you will be fired. Is it a chance worth taking? You have several things to consider.

How Does Your Record Relate To The Job
For Which You Are Applying?

If your job goal has something to do with your past crimes, you may have to put your goals on hold. For instance, if you have a good head for money and you previously embezzled funds from

your employer, you can see why you might not get hired to work for a bank. The more distance you can put between your crime and your aspirations, the better.

Does The Job Require A Lot Of Responsibility And Trust?

It is a sure bet, if there is a lot of responsibility involved, the employer will check you out, and not just your criminal history. They will want to check with former employers, employment dates, references — you name it.

If you want to avoid any investigation, aim for entry-level type jobs. The interview will be minimal for this type of job and they might not even ask about your history.

Will You Be Working With Others?

Just as responsibility calls for a more thorough background check, so would working with other people: the elderly, children, patients. If your record has anything to do with having endangered others, you can be confident you should look into a new field.

Your background will probably be checked when you have more responsibility, pay, and contact with other people. With some companies, it is just a matter of policy.

If the job is temporary, chances are there won't be an in-depth check on your background. All the better, you might think, but be warned. The longer you work for a company, the more danger of the truth coming out about your past.

What If Your Parole Officer Checks Up On You?

What about your parole supervision? How will your probation officer check up on you? What if he or she lets the cat out of the bag by checking on you at work? It is very important that you have an understanding with your parole officer on how this will be handled. Somewhere down the line, you could be assigned a new P.O. Come to an understanding with him or her, as well. This is your future at stake. It is important to get it straight from the start.

To Tell Or Not To Tell

If you are honest about your record, you may get the job. Honesty may indicate that you are probably serious about turning your life around. But, *in all honesty*, when you tell the truth, you run the risk of rejection.

If you decide not to tell, you will live in constant fear of somebody finding out. You will have to watch what you say and be careful not to give yourself away. That can drive you crazy! If you are found out, you could lose everything: your income, self esteem, and future jobs.

Weigh the positives and negatives and decide what is best for you and what risks you are

willing to take. It is not easy. Whatever you decide, be prepared for the consequences. It is obviously your choice, but we recommend putting all the cards on the table and starting fresh without any time bombs hanging around.

If You Tell

Talking about your record will be the hardest part. If you decide to tell the truth about your record, try to be honest, direct, and calm. Be the first to bring it up if it looks like the interviewer isn't going to. Get to the point. For example:

"In 1993 I was convicted of _____ and served _____ years in the state penitentiary. I am not proud of this time in my life but I take full responsibility for my actions. This time in my life has taught me to evaluate my priorities. I am no longer doing _____ or _____. I am highly motivated to prove myself and fully intend to turn my life around.
I understand it would be hard for you to put yourself in my shoes, and that you would hesitate to believe in me. I can tell you, I am serious about wanting to work for you and I will work very hard to prove myself. You can watch me extra closely. You can keep me on probation. I want the opportunity to prove myself and I am willing to do anything to do that."

Approach your circumstances like this story. Your goal is to get the interviewer to understand your situation and make him or her believe that you have put this behind you. Your goal should not be to make the interviewer feel sorry for you. If the employer does not believe that you have put this behind you, you will not get the job.

End your story on a positive note. Point out what you have done to better yourself since you were incarcerated. Have you gone back to school or received more training? Are you attending church? Do you have better relationships with loved ones?

The goal is to get the interviewer to understand your motivation to have a brighter future. Everyone has done something they wish they hadn't and everyone deserves a second chance.
Adjust this story to your own situation and practice saying it to someone.

What About Money?

How do you cope with the question of money if it comes up early in the interview? First, don't get flustered or embarrassed. And control the urge to blurt out a figure at this point. You can respond with, "Mr. Brown, I don't mind discussing salary, but I'd rather do it later into the interview. I'd like to know more about the duties and responsibilities of the position, as I'm sure you'd like to know more about me."

Don't base your starting salary on your previous earnings. The key factors should be the responsibilities of the new job and what you are worth to the company.
Should the final salary offered be less than you anticipated, and you really want the job, try to

get a commitment for a raise within a specified time. Again, a lot depends on your particular situation. Do you have specialized skills that are in demand? Do you have a good educational background?

The Interview is Over—Now What?

When the interview is almost over, if you want the job, tell the employer. Tell her you enjoyed learning more about the job and would like the position. If the employer is unable to offer you the job right then, ask her when you can expect to hear from her. Thank her and follow up with a thank-you letter.

Go into every interview knowing you are going to give it your best shot. If it doesn't work out, it is not the end of the world. Don't be too hard on yourself. You may feel bad but this interview will not stop the planet from rotating. Consider every interview good practice for the next one. You learn a little each time and your confidence builds with each interview.

Overcoming Rejection

You were turned down again. You are feeling like the walls are closing in and you want to scream. You are very angry. Now wait a minute. What happens when you feel this way? Maybe you slip back into the behavior that got you into trouble in the first place. You don't want to wind up in prison again, so calm down and collect yourself.

If you think finding a job is going to be a piece of cake, pop that bubble now. Your history is without a doubt the biggest and toughest hurdle you will ever have to overcome. It is not going to be easy. Time and time again, you may be rejected because you are considered a risky investment.

Every time you are knocked down, pick yourself up again. After every experience, ask yourself, "What can I learn from this experience that will help me in the future?"

Think about your interview. How did you do? Did any questions throw you? Could you have done something differently? Did you give a pretty good answer to one or two of the questions? If so, now is the time to write it down. You will gain something from each interview, and that is how you get better. Do not give up. You need the will to survive and the courage to get back in the race again. After each interview, you will be stronger and better prepared.

Thank-You Letters

You have one more chore to do after your interview. It is a small task, but it can improve your chances for a second interview. It can also give you an opportunity to add to or emphasize any points you may have left out the first time. It is simple and done too infrequently, making it all the more effective. Type or hand write a thank you letter to the person who interviewed you. This is the only time a handwritten note is acceptable. It should be brief and should include the following points:

√   You appreciated his or her time.
√   You are interested in the company and the position.
√   You are confident that you can handle the responsibilities of the position.
√   List one or two of the most important specifications of the job and point out your qualifications.
√   Offer to provide further information if needed.

For example:

Jeff Stratton
555 East Main Street
Charleston, N.C. 90121
(412) 555-2402

January 6, 1999

Mr. Scott Eubank
Manager
Jones Trucking
700 West Main Street
Charleston, N.C. 90122

Dear Mr. Eubank,

Thank you for seeing me last Thursday. I enjoyed meeting you and having the opportunity to discuss my qualifications for the driver position. You may recall that I have three years driving experience and have my certification.

I hope I answered all of your questions. Please feel free to call me if you need more information. I am very interested in working for you and hope to hear from you soon.

Sincerely,

Jeff Stratton

Chapter 11

It's 10 o'clock.
Do You Know Where Your Resume Is?

After a month of reading ads, writing letters, mailing resumes, making phone calls and, having interviews, enough information will flow through you to fill a sizable filing cabinet. If you don't keep a daily record of your activities, you will soon be lost.

It is especially important to keep track of where you send your resumes. In order to follow up effectively, you have to know where they are. Unless you keep accurate records, you will be hopelessly confused about where you have been, whom you have seen, and what you have said.

Tracking Techniques

A good way to keep track of your activities is to start a file folder for every company you contact. Into this folder, place copies of:

- letters you write and receive
- business cards and names of contact persons
- company literature
- annual reports
- notes from phone conversations
- impressions of people and places
- notes from interviews
- any other data relating to your job hunt.

When you receive a call or a letter from a company or a callback for a second interview, just open the appropriate folder to help you remember them. You can also bring this folder to the interview to refer to notes that you have made about the company. It is impossible to look for a job without keeping records.

Looking Forward

"You're hired. Report for work Monday." You have finally heard the words you have been hoping for all these weeks or months. Now that you have accepted an offer and are ready for that first day on the job, you have made a commitment to give your best efforts to your new employer. This means that you have to develop good work habits.

Here are some tips to make the most of your new job:

- Be on time for work every day and don't go over the time allotted for breaks and lunch. Punctuality is a major factor when it comes to promotions and raises. It is also one of the major causes for being fired — especially for new hires.

- Be eager to learn. Look for ways to make yourself more valuable to your employer. One way is to show him or her how dependable you are or that you are interested in taking on more responsibility.

- Try to get along with everyone including coworkers and customers.

- Don't criticize fellow workers or supervisors behind their backs. You never know when someone will repeat what you have said.

- Don't take days off unnecessarily. This practice will cause negative remarks to be made in your performance file. You may think that your absence won't cause any serious harm to the office or shop, but you were hired because you were needed.

- Try not to get down if parts of your job are unpleasant or unchallenging. Everyone has to pay their dues with the grunt work in the beginning.

- Show that you are interested in learning more whenever you can. Ask your boss if there is something extra you can do to become better at your job.

If you do well on your job, you will be able to look forward to gaining more skills and experience that could lead to a promotion. This will put you in the position to advance either in this job or a new one.

Working as a dishwasher in a restaurant could eventually lead to being a restaurant manager. Working as a car mechanic could turn into a job as a shop supervisor. By improving your skills you become more valuable, not only to your current boss, but to any future employers you have down the road.

Take advantage of every training opportunity you can. Are there any apprenticeships you can take advantage of? About 100,000 new apprenticeships are registered each year. Workers who have undergone these types of programs have advantages over other employees. They are normally considered better trained and better able to do the job.

Apprenticeship programs have different requirements. You may have to meet an age, education (many require a high school diploma or G.E.D.), aptitude (reading, writing, and math skills), or physical condition requirement.

Dead End Career? Shift Your Gear

Get all the experience you can and try to stick with your new job for at least a year. If you keep moving from one job to another, you'll look like an unstable employee. Employers don't like this. The new job may not be what you expected, but it is important that you start exhibiting a steady work habit.

Give it at least a year. If after a year you decide the job isn't right for you, you can start looking for a new position. Then, in an interview for your next job, when the employer asks why you left after only a year, you can say, "A year gave me enough time to learn what I needed from that position. I am ready for more challenging experiences."

Be prepared to answer what skills you learned and why you felt it wasn't necessary to stay there any longer. Employers want answers to everything.

Look Before You Leap

If you decide to move on, you may start wondering where to go. Before you look for a new career, you first have to take a good look at yourself. You have to know the real reasons for your dissatisfaction.

Finding lasting satisfaction takes more than just getting another job. Those who move from one company to another without analyzing their motives and skills are doomed to end up in jobs for which they are unqualified, unsuited, and unhappy. They become "job hoppers."

Before you decide to move into a new career, ask yourself some important questions.

- Am I really dissatisfied with my work, or is it my employer that's the problem?
- Am I clear in my mind about what I really want to do?
- Am I sure it is my work that's the problem or is it something more personal?
- Nothing is certain. If I make a move, am I prepared for the personal and financial risks?
- Would I have to go back to school for further education or training for my new career?
- Of my present skills and abilities, how many can be applied to a new career field?
- Have I researched my new job choice thoroughly?
- Am I willing to start at the bottom in a new career? Am I prepared for the limited amount of responsibilities and the low income I may earn?
- Have I considered all my options?

If you have trouble answering any of these questions, it may be helpful to go back to Chapter 2 of this book and review/revise your lists: what are your strengths, weaknesses, interests, and what do you want to do?

In Summary

If you sincerely want to change and become a success in life, you have every opportunity to do so. The resources are out there to help you.

- If you can get more education and training while inside, get it; otherwise prepare to do it when you get out.
- Find that person who will help you begin your job search, the person who will help you create a good resume and will help you establish a job search goal.
- Look in the Government Listings for the agencies mentioned throughout this book.
- Surround yourself with a lot of people who will help you and keep you motivated.
- Don't give up. Prepare yourself for an uphill battle.
- Learn from your experiences. Gain something from each interview.
- Practice what to say and how to say it.
- Once you have found a job, work hard and learn as much as you can.
- Take advantage of every training opportunity available.
- Be eager to learn.
- Maintain a positive attitude.

Remember, education and training are probably the two most important factors that will help you get a job and keep it. And keeping a job is the most important way to keep yourself out of trouble.

Training may lead to promotions and more responsibility. Work your way up the ladder. Through job training, experience and lots of hard work, you not only increase your self esteem, but you become a productive, working person in society, and an asset to your company.

Millions have made new lives for themselves. You can too. Just go do it.

NOTES

NOTES

FROM PAROLE TO PAYROLL

For the ex-offender, finding a job is one of the most difficult, and important, steps toward building a new and productive life. How do you sell yourself? How do you make the most of what many employers see as a devastating mistake? Do you tell them you spent time in prison? How do you convince them they can trust you? Where do you even begin looking for a job? This comprehensive, concise, three part job search series is ideal for introducing job seekers to the latest information and techniques in selecting a career and getting a job. Designed specifically for ex-offenders, this series is loaded with solid content, informative interviews, helpful tips, and colorful graphics. © 1997.

from parole to payroll

finding a job

resumes and job applications

the interview

CAMBRIDGE EDUCATIONAL®

FROM PAROLE TO PAYROLL: FINDING A JOB
CCP0271V   VHS $98.00

This lively program discusses the many ways ex-offenders can find job openings using both unconventional job search methods (networking, informational interviews, the internet, yellow pages, etc.) and conventional job search methods (want ads, resumes, job applications, state & private employment services, etc.). Discusses the advantages and disadvantages of each method and, more importantly, which job search methods are most likely to work for ex-offenders. Emphasis is put on using ALL available methods in a job search but specific tips and pointers are given to help the ex-offender. Interviews with parole officers, job search specialists, and ex-offenders who have found a job illustrate the best and quickest ways to get a job! One 22-minute videocassette.

FROM PAROLE TO PAYROLL: RESUMES AND JOB APPLICATIONS
CCP0272V   VHS $98.00

This program shows how parolees can use resumes and job applications most effectively as an integral tool in the job search process. The video not only discusses the purpose and place of the resume and job application, but also, how the ex-offender can use these tools to overcome the issues involved in finding a job. The types of resumes are discussed and emphasis is placed on which ones are most useful to the ex-offender and why. Offers specific ways to deal with time gaps, prison education programs, and much more. One 19-minute videocassette.

FROM PAROLE TO PAYROLL: THE JOB INTERVIEW
CCP0273V   VHS $98.00

What are the most common mistakes ex-offenders make in interviewing for a job? What can the parolee do to answer difficult questions relating to his or her past? The interview is the most crucial stage in the job search process for the ex-offender. The interview results in a job offer, or it does not... no second chances. This program covers preparing for your interview, dressing for your interview, using body language to your advantage, articulating your skills and abilities, answering difficult questions, and handling salary and benefit issues. Emphasis is placed on being prepared in this thorough and comprehensive coverage of the most important step in the job search process. One 15-minute videocassette.

CAREER S.E.L.F. ASSESSMENT
Finding a Job That Works for You
CCP0275V   **VHS**   **$89.00**

STOP! Before you start looking for a job, take a good look at your S.E.L.F. This program shows how to assess your Strengths, Experiences, Lifestyle, and the way you Function best. Each of these elements are part of your S.E.L.F. and all should be considered when choosing a career. This program stresses the importance of knowing who you are and what direction you want your life to take before fitting your S.E.L.F. into the world of work. The key to finding the right job or career is asking your S.E.L.F. the right questions. This entertaining program discusses the questions job seekers need to answer. One 32-minute videocassette. © 1996.

RESUME EXPRESS
CCP0237W   **Windows CD-ROM**   **$99.00**
CCP0237CM   **Macintosh CD-ROM**   **$99.00**

How did resumes become such an important part of the job search process? What kind of resume will present my level of experience in the best light? How do I write a resume—and how do I use it? This state-of-the-art multimedia CD-ROM not only answers these and other questions, but it also provides an easy-to-use, resume-writing program from which users can print high quality resumes and cover letters to market their skills. Using videos, narration, and colorful on-screen graphics, users learn the history of resumes, what employers look for in a resume, how to write a resume for any level of job experience, and what information should be included. From the Dynamo List, they learn about "action" words which employers look for in resumes. Additionally, they learn what is meant by "customizing" a resume and how they can use their resumes to target different kinds of job. Users may then enter a resume writing feature in which they create a customized, attention-grabbing resume. Utilizing a easy-to-use data entry feature, users enter their Job Objective, Education, Work Experience, Qualifications, Skills, and Accomplishments. The program assembles their data to be printed in Chronological, Functional, or Combination style. A word processing feature gives users the ability to make quick editorial and design changes, such as fonts and font sizes, headings, format and more. Using the strengths of the interactive multimedia environment, this exceptional program goes beyond the limits of other resume writing programs by not only teaching users about resume writing, but also taking them step-by-step through the resume creation process. One CD-ROM and documentation. © 1995.

Requirements: MPC Level 2—4 MB RAM (8 MB RAM recommended), 160 MB Hard Drive, CD-ROM drive, and color monitor.

THE IDEAL RESUME
CCP0307V   **VHS**   **$79.95**

This concise, informative program shows the viewer how to effectively use a resume as an advertisement selling the job seeker's achievements, skills and abilities.

Appropriate for adults and youth from the first time job hunter to the career changer, this video covers the purpose of the resume, styles of resumes (chronological, skills, and combination), what information to include and not include, and what favorably catches the employer's eye. Does a great job in not only explaining how to create a resume, but also how to utilize the resume most advantageously in a self-directed job search. The program shows how to use electronic resumes and how and where to post them on the internet. Illustrates how to use a resume effectively in conjunction with cover letters to get noticed and to get an interview! One 20-minute videocassette. © 1996.

ACE THE INTERVIEW
The Multimedia Job Interview Guide
CCP0295C   **CD-ROM**   **$99.00**

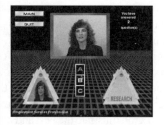

Job hunting has never been easy, especially for young adults who have limited experience. There are two keys to finding a decent job: 1) you must market yourself intelligently, and 2) you must be committed to investing the required time and effort into learning the elements of a successful job search. By combining the power of the computer with full-motion video, audio, graphics and text, **Ace The Interview** provides an entertaining and creative approach to learning about the different stages of the job interview process. It also increases content understanding through a series of games and interview examples. Users are guided through a self-directed series of interview scenarios and expert tips. This program is divided into three sections: Doing your homework (preparation and personal presentation); In The Spotlight (the interview process); and Follow-up. **Ace The Interview** is designed to improve the user's knowledge of interviewing techniques. It presents video scenarios that show realistic portrayals of the skills being taught. It will attract users to experience responses to the problem situations portrayed. It will also expose users to a variety of situations and provide opportunities for learner input through the interactive format. This interactive approach of **Ace The Interview** provides flexible instructional strategies to meet the needs of a wide range of learning styles. One compact disc containing both Windows and Macintosh versions. © 1996.

System Requirements: Windows version—4MB RAM, color monitor, sound card, and a double speed CD-ROM drive. Macintosh version—System 7.1 or higher, 4MB RAM, color monitor, and a double speed CD-ROM drive.

COMMON MISTAKES PEOPLE MAKE IN INTERVIEWS
CCP0225V   VHS $79.95

Before you even walk through the front door of a company for an interview, you better know a few things: what the business is all about; how to stay cool under pressure; and what your thoughts are about working with people of different race and gender. After all, an interview is a serious conversation about business, how you react to stress and what kind of person you really are. Common Mistakes People Make in Interviews is an interesting and effective program that helps job seekers anticipate what interviewers are looking for so they do not make the common mistakes most job seekers make. Creatively using a wrong way/right way format, this program illustrates potential pitfalls in the job interview and helps job seekers overcome them. Common Mistakes People Make in Interviews is a gold mine of informative techniques to show job seekers how to do well in the interview and GET THE JOB OFFER! Perfect for job search agencies, libraries, career-oriented classes or anyone interested in acing the interview. One 40-minute videocassette. © 1995.

EXTRAORDINARY ANSWERS TO COMMON INTERVIEW QUESTIONS
CCP0238V   VHS $79.95

"What can you tell me about yourself?" "Why do you want to leave your current job?" "What are your strengths and weaknesses?" "What could you bring to this job?" Let's face it, these are common questions, but they are tough! You can bet, most employers are going to ask these and several other questions, but most job seekers are not going to answer them well. This doesn't have to be the case. This well-thought-out program uses a fun quiz show format to help job seekers recognize good and bad answers to common interview questions. Each segment is followed by advice from career experts on how to articulate great answers. All it takes is preparation. If job seeker's prepare well for the interview, they can approach any question with confidence and success. *Extraordinary Answers* outlines key principles to effective interviewing and then applies those principles to numerous questions interviewers are most likely to ask. Perfect for anyone about to be interviewed—whether it's their first time or their twentieth. No job seeker should leave for their interview without Learning the *Extraordinary Answers*! Contents: One 30-minute videocassette. © 1995.

INFORMATION SUPERHIGHWAY SERIES

CONNECT ON THE NET
Finding a Job on the Internet
CCP0228V   VHS $79.95

Businesses everywhere are taking to the Highway. The Internet helps businesses run their operations smarter, more timely and more cost efficient—especially when it comes to hiring. If you are looking for a job, the Internet provides a variety of tools to assist in preparing and searching for employment. Viewers learn how to use both traditional and nontraditional job search strategies such as networking, browsing through job listings or posting their resume, as they navigate through job search directories and bulletin boards on the Internet. Job-Net is an easy-to-use, timely production that contains lively discussions about job search techniques found on the Information Superhighway. The smartest resource to date for employers and job seekers. One 30-minute videocassette. © 1995.

YOUR FIRST CRUISE
A Beginner's Guide to the Internet
CCP0229V   VHS $79.95

Teachers and students can find a wealth of useful information through this video. Very soon all K-12 schools, and colleges and universities will be online. But, what do users do once they get there? Your First Cruise is the most understandable and comprehensive program to describe what the Internet is, how it was developed, access requirements, popular features and how to navigate through the system once you get there. Your First Cruise takes the mystery away by explaining what services are offered and how to obtain the connection that will meet your needs. Communicating with anyone, anywhere, at anytime in the world is now possible at the click of a mouse. Take the step. Hop aboard and let Your First Cruise show your students the world. One 30-minute videocassette. © 1995.

*** BUY THE SERIES AND SAVE! ***

CCP0230SV   Information Superhighway Series, VHS . . . $149.95

TOUGH TIMES JOB STRATEGIES

Where have all the jobs gone? What can I do to find a job and ensure my future employment? This two-part video series examines the effects of increased global competition, technological innovation, changing demographics, and other factors influencing today's job market. Viewers learn not only the effects of these changes on the kinds of jobs that are available, but also how they can plan a strategy to gain the knowledge and experience necessary to stay employed in the future.

Tough Times: Finding the Jobs
CCP0129V-D . . . $69.95

Tough Times: Making the Most of Your Job
CCP0130V-D . . . $69.95

This informative video explains how worldwide changes and trends affect the job market on a local level. Viewers learn the importance of researching these effects on the area in which they are seeking employment and examining economic development strategies for their regions and states. They are shown the benefits of researching various industries to determine which are experiencing growth and which are declining and are encouraged to acquire the skills needed for entry level employment in the most promising job markets. Viewers realize that in today's job market, they are responsible for their own career development and that each job should be assessed not only for the immediate opportunities offered, but also for its qualities as a stepping stone to a secure future. One 30-minute videocassette. © 1993.

No longer is it enough for employees to show up at work, do their jobs and go home. Today's job market requires individuals to have many attributes and to continuously work to expand their skills and knowledge. This important lesson teaches entry level employees the importance of making the most of their present jobs. Viewers see how their jobs can be used to advance their careers, either within or outside their companies. Communication skills, flexibility, company knowledge and the willingness to take on extra responsibilities and learn new skills are stressed as stepping stones to career advancement and job security. This valuable program is a must-see for anyone seeking or currently employed in an entry level position. One 30-minute videocassette. © 1993.

*** Order the Series and Save! ***

CCP0131SV   Tough Times Job Strategies Series, VHS . . . $129.00

CAMBRIDGE JOB SEARCH POSTERS

Enhance the decor of any environment with this richly colored and dramatically illustrated set of prints. Each depicts a basic concept of an effective, self-directed job search including networking, interviewing, resume preparation, formulating cover letters and much more! These handsomely designed prints are informational as well as inspirational and are perfect for decorating classrooms, waiting areas, offices and meeting rooms. An ideal means for motivating job seekers to begin applying themselves. Contents: Ten 17" x 22" posters and lithographs. © 1992.

CCPOST4	Job Search Poster Series	$49.95
	Individual Poster	$5.95
CCPOST4L	Job Search Poster Series Laminated	$49.95
	Individual Laminated Poster	$7.95
CCPOST4F	Job Search Poster Series Framed	$379.00
	Individual Framed Poster	$39.95

CCPOST41-D	Networking
CCPOST42-D	Thank You Notes
CCPOST43-D	Cover Letters
CCPOST44-D	Functional Resumes
CCPOST45-D	Mom & Pop Still Have a Lot to Offer
CCPOST46-D	Job Applications
CCPOST47-D	Chronological Resumes
CCPOST48-D	Preparing for A Job Interview
CCPOST49-D	Why Should I Hire You?
CCPOST410-D	Informational Interviews

CAMBRIDGE MOTIVATIONAL JOB SEARCH POSTERS

These colorful motivational posters create a positive attitude in any classroom, employment center or guidance office. Dramatic photography and stimulating slogans of positive reinforcement cover goal setting, risk taking, confidence, networking, opportunities, achievements, flexibility, and maintaining a positive attitude. Ten 17" x 22" full-color posters. © 1995.

CCPOST24	Motivational Job Search Poster Series	$49.95
	Individual Poster	$5.95
CCPOST24L	Motivational Job Search Series Laminated	$59.95
	Individual Laminated Poster	$7.95
CCPOST24F	Motivational Job Search Series Framed	$379.00
	Individual Framed Poster	$39.95

CCPOST231	Risk
CCPOST241	Career vs. Job
CCPOST242	Motivation & Confidence
CCPOST243	Job Satisfaction
CCPOST235	Goals
CCPOST244	Networking
CCPOST237	Opportunities
CCPOST238	Achievements
CCPOST239	Flexibility
CCPOST2310	Positive Attitude

To order call:
1 304 744-9323
1 800 468-4227

To order FAX:
1 304 744-9351
1 800 FAX-ON US

CAMBRIDGE EDUCATIONAL
P.O. BOX 2153
CHARLESTON, WV 25328

QTY	TITLE	ORDER #	COST	TOTAL
	BOOKS			
	The Ex-Offender's Job Search Companion	CCP0315	$9.95	
	VIDEOCASSETTES			
	From Parole to Payroll: Finding A Job	CCP0271V	$98.00	
	From Parole to Payroll: Resumes & Job Applications	CCP0272V	$98.00	
	From Parole to Payroll: The Job Interview	CCP0273V	$98.00	
	From Parole to Payroll Series	CCP0274SV	$275.00	
	The Ideal Resume	CCP0307V	$79.95	
	Common Mistakes People Make In Interviews	CCP0225V	$79.95	
	Extraordinary Answers to Common Interview Questions	CCP0238V	$79.95	
	Information Superhighway Series	CCP0230SV	$149.95	
	Career S.E.L.F. Assessment	CCP0275V	$89.00	
	Tough Times Job Strategies Series	CCP0131SV	$129.00	
	CD-ROMs			
	Ace the Interview	CCP0295C	$99.00	
	Resume Express—Windows Resume Express—Macintosh	CCP0237W CCP0237M	$99.00 $99.00	
	POSTERS			
	Job Search Poster Series—Laminated	CCPOST4L	$59.95	
	Motivational Job Search Poster Series—Laminated	CCPOST24L	$59.95	
	Please Call for Shipping Info			